EASY HALLOWEEN COSTUMES FOR CHILDREN

by Leila Albala

THIRD REVISED EDITION

This book is affectionately dedicated to all Canadian and American children. May they find the magic and fantasy of a safe and happy Halloween.

Martin and Rina

ALPEL, Chambly, Quebec, Canada

EASY HALLOWEEN COSTUMES FOR CHILDREN
by Leila Albala

THIRD REVISED EDITION

Published by: ALPEL, P.O.Box 203,
Chambly, Quebec, Canada J3L 4B3

Other books by Leila Albala:
Easy Sewing for Infants (70 patterns)
Easy Sewing for Children (75 patterns)
Easy Sewing for Adults (78 patterns)

Canadian Cataloguing in Publication Data

Albala, Leila
  Easy Halloween costumes for children

3rd ed.
Includes index.
ISBN 0-9691932-8-9

1. Children--Costumes. 2. Halloween.
3. Dressmaking--Patterns. 4. Children's
clothing. I. Title.

TT633.A43 1987   646.4'706   C87-090061-7

Printed in Canada   Reprinted in August 1989.

WHAT THEY SAY ABOUT "EASY HALLOWEEN COSTUMES"...

"A real lifesaver." (Creative Product News)

"A book to rescue you." (The Houston Post)

"Leila Albala's EASY HALLOWEEN COSTUMES FOR CHILDREN could very well be renamed HALLOWEEN WITHOUT HASSLE for making this occasion fun for adults as well as children. This handy manual lends creative assistance and a much needed alternative to store-bought costumes." (Vogue Patterns)

"Clever ideas. Indispensable holiday item." (Booklist)

"Gold-mine of information." (Canadian Book Review Annual)

"The book is a delight, a manual of how to dress excited little trick-or-treaters creatively without spending bundles of cash or time. The ideas are incredible. Just reading the book excites the imagination." (Calgary Herald)

"Delightful drawings, original ideas." (Joan Watson, Syndicated Consumer Columnist)

"Creative and fun. Real treat for the kids." (The Sentinel-Review)

"Clear instructions and patterns for novice and experienced guardians of this frightful night of fall fancy." (Chicago Sun-Times)

"A lifetime selection of costumes. Cute illustrations. And the language IS easy to understand." (Brampton Times)

"Clear and concise." (The Times-News)

"The most complete publication for at-home costumers." (The Edmonton Journal)

"Delightful but - more important - useful manual for Halloween-distressed mothers. A comfort to have on hand." (Starlight)

"Turn your child's Halloween into a big treat." (Farm Woman)

"Incredible ideas." (Canadian Shopper)

"Comprehensive handbook for dressing up kids with imagination and style. Simple and straightforward with easy-to-follow instructions and patterns." (The Windsor Star)

"If you want to add some fun and creativity to this year's costume, Leila Albala's book can be a great help." (The Toronto Star)

"Fret not. EASY HALLOWEEN COSTUMES FOR CHILDREN could guide parents through the annual costume hassle." (The Montreal Gazette)

"We could go on and on forever extolling the wonderful virtues of this exciting book." (Kids Toronto)

"Wonderful! Excellent line drawings." (Vicki Lansky, author of "Feed Me I'm Yours")

ACKNOWLEDGEMENTS

I sincerely thank the following organizations for their cooperation:

Canada Safety Council
1765 St Laurent Blvd.
Ottawa, Canada K1G 3V4

National Safety Council
444 North Michigan Avenue
Chicago, Illinois
USA 60611

UNICEF Canada
443 Mt. Pleasant Road
Toronto, Ontario
M4S 2L8

United States Committee for UNICEF
331 East 38th Street
New York, N.Y.
USA 10016

(All photographs in this book by Elie Albala)

ANGELICA, THE CAT

ANGELICA, THE BEDOUIN
ALBERT, THE KNIGHT
RINA, THE GNOME

VISUAL COSTUME INDEX

Costume number under each design.
(Page number in parenthesis.)

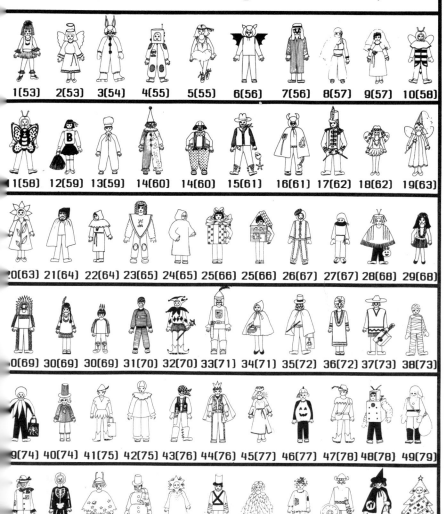

1(53) 2(53) 3(54) 4(55) 5(55) 6(56) 7(56) 8(57) 9(57) 10(58)

11(58) 12(59) 13(59) 14(60) 14(60) 15(61) 16(61) 17(62) 18(62) 19(63)

20(63) 21(64) 22(64) 23(65) 24(65) 25(66) 25(66) 26(67) 27(67) 28(68) 29(68)

30(69) 30(69) 30(69) 31(70) 32(70) 33(71) 34(71) 35(72) 36(72) 37(73) 38(73)

39(74) 40(74) 41(75) 42(75) 43(76) 44(76) 45(77) 46(77) 47(78) 48(78) 49(79)

50(79) 51(80) 52(80) 53(81) 54(81) 55(82) 56(82) 57(83) 58(83) 59(84) 60(84)

5

CONTENTS

TO THE READER

Every October, the anticipation of Halloween brings a thrilled smile to youngsters but creates a big headache for moms. The treat is for the kid, the trick for the mom, trying to find costume ideas and patterns. To the rescue comes this pattern book with dozens of easy, inexpensive, and innovative costumes.

When I came to Canada from Finland in 1973, I had never heard of Halloween. Instantly fascinated by costumed trick-or-treaters, I wished to be a child again and join them. Years later, realizing I was not alone in frantically improvising costumes at the last minute for my own children, I became a 'Halloween detective'. I was determined to collect facts and ideas to learn more about the background, customs and costumes of this yearly celebration. I wrote this book to share that knowledge with my readers.

Including mostly simplified costumes that are easy to create, yet allow creativity, this book also has several simple, no-sew costumes and last-minute designs so that the children can participate in creating them. Show this book to children, they will love the cute illustrations and will immediately pick out their favorite costumes for many a Halloween. Traditional Halloween costumes are all here and a whole lot more. I have added a brief history, safety tips, and other entertaining and useful facts and ideas, written so that children too, will find this book interesting.

Although titled for Halloween, the costumes and accessories in this book are useful for other costume occasions and school plays, too. Use your imagination to modify any costume, making it unique and to suit your taste, needs and budget. Children need traditions and they love costumes. Put it all together and you have a winning combination. Make memories together. Keep it simple and have fun! May you enjoy this book for years to come.

HALLOWEEN'S HISTORY

Halloween, or Allhallows Eve, a yearly celebration held on the evening of October 31, has evolved from blended traditions of several cultures over thousands of years. Most symbols and customs of modern Halloween originate from ancient Celtic and Roman festivities.

The Celtic tribes that lived more than two thousand years ago, in what is now Great Britain and Ireland, celebrated November 1 as the first day of winter, cold and darkness, and the beginning of a New Year. New Year's Eve, October 31, was the festival of Samhain, Celtic Lord of death. The Druid priests of the Celts believed that the ghosts, goblins and other creatures of dark came to life to wander freely on that day only, with witches riding broomsticks across the sky to meet the devil. The Druids, dressed in masks and costumes to disguise themselves against harmful spirits, went from house to house begging for food and firewood for the Samhain festivities. Huge bonfires were lit on hilltops of Celtic Britain to drive away evil spirits. In every home, the hearth fires were extinguished and then relit by burning coals carried from the sacred fires. Turnips and potatoes were carved into jack-o'-lanterns and, lit by a glowing coal inside, were carried door-to-door to light the way for wandering souls and to scare away witches and goblins.

According to an old Irish legend, jack-o'-lanterns were named for a drunk and mean man called Jack. He could not enter heaven because he was too wicked, and was barred even from hell because he had played tricks on the devil. As a result, Jack was condemned to walk the earth forever, a lost soul with only a lantern to light his way, until Judgment Day.

When the Romans who, according to the Julian calendar, had their New Year on January 1, conquered Britain in the first century A.D., they regarded this Celtic holiday as barbaric and attempted to civilize it by substituting some of their own festivities. Roman autumn festivals were combined with the Celtic festival of Samhain. Celtic harvest traditions with bonfires, parades and lanterns were adopted by Romans and, centuries later, Christians adopted the Roman celebrations.

In the 800's, hoping to erase the pagan aspects from the already popular harvest celebration, the Church sanctified the ancient Celtic holiday by establishing All Hallows' (Saints') Day on November 1. Thereby the people could continue a festival they had celebrated before becoming Christians. Many of the traditional customs of the Celts survived and were celebrated on the night before All Hallows' Day.

The name Halloween comes from "Hallows' Eve", the evening before All Hallows', or All Saints' Day, when all saints are honored. In medieval times, elaborately dressed statues of saints were paraded that day with parishioners dressed in costumes of saints and biblical characters.

Brought to this continent by the great wave of Irish and Scottish immigrants in the 1800's, Halloween was an occasion for hayrides, bonfires, ghost stories and practical jokes. Gradually this joyous day evolved into the event as it is now known and celebrated in the United States and Canada. Many communities nowadays sponsor bonfires, dances, costume parades and other entertainment to celebrate Halloween. Irish turnips were replaced with pumpkins for jack-o'-lanterns, while costumes and merry trick-o'-treating are humorous historical reminders of ancient ghoulish traditions.

MAKE HALLOWEEN SAFE

There is no real trick to making Halloween a treat for the entire family. However, the responsibility for a safe and enjoyable occasion is shared by adults and children. The dangers are not from witches or spirits but rather from falls, pedestrian and car accidents, and deliberate Halloween hazards. These tips (courtesy of National Safety Council, Chicago, Illinois, USA, and Canada Safety Council, Ottawa) will help your children have their fun and eat their candy, too.

Preparing your children

Costume

Design or buy the costumes so that children can easily walk without tripping, entangling their feet or falling.

Costumes should be lightweight and fit properly, yet large enough so that warm clothing can be worn underneath if it's cold outside.

Children should wear comfortable, well-fitted shoes. Clumsy and heavy shoes and mom's high-heels contribute to sore feet, falls, spilled treats, and tears.

Wigs, beards, whiskers and hats should be fastened securely and designed so that they don't get into youngsters' eyes, obscuring vision.

Use light colors, decals or reflective tape so that youngsters are visible at night to motorists. (Reflective tape can be purchased at most hardware, bicycle and sporting-goods stores; any leftover can be put onto schoolbags, rainwear and bicycles.)

Fires do not take vacations on Halloween night. Buy flame-resistant costumes or make them from flame-resistant material. Look for the markings on the label, box or material. To prevent clothing ignition, handmade costumes can be flame-proofed: dip fabrics into a solution of 2.5 L (2 quarts) warm water, 200 mL (7 ounces) borax and 85 mL (3 ounces) boric acid; drip dry and iron. To preserve flame resistancy, this must be repeated after each washing.

Face design

Masks with narrow eye slits obscure a child's ability to see oncoming traffic, curbs, or obstructed pathways. Facial makeup is safer, more fun and more comfortable. If masks are worn, they should have openings for the nose and mouth, and large eye holes to allow full vision. Instruct children to wear the mask on top of the head when walking and pull it over the face only when reaching the location.

When buying special Halloween makeup, check for packages that are labeled "Made with U.S. Approved Color Additivies", "Laboratory Tested", "Meets Federal Standards for Cosmetics", or "Non-Toxic". Most manufacturers list ingredients and/or chemical analysis on packages. Follow manufacturer's instructions for application and removal.

Professional makeup crayons are available at costume shops and theatrical supply stores. Or use regular makeup, lipstick, blush, brow pencils, and eye shadows. Or use homemade makeup; see recipe on page 32.

Adults should supervise the application of makeup for young children. Keep makeup out of eyes. Children can draw pictures of the face they want parents to design on them. Types of faces can include witches, goblins, ghosts, pirates, Indians, clowns, devils, hobos, cartoon characters or popular television or movie characters.

Accessories

Swords, magic wands, and other props must be harmless and made from cardboard or other pliable material that will not cause injury if your child tumbles onto them. Never allow children to carry real knives or other sharp objects.

Bags carried by youngsters should be light-colored or trimmed with reflective tape or decals if trick-or-treaters are allowed out after dark.

Carrying flashlights will help children see better and be seen more clearly. Never allow anyone to walk using a flame for a light.

Before they go

Plan and discuss the route trick-or-treaters intend to follow. Instruct children to go only into familiar neighborhoods and choose well-lit streets.

Do not allow children to travel alone or unsupervised. Young children should be accompanied by an adult or responsible older child.

Set a time limit if children are old enough to go with their friends. Know the names of the companions older children are with. Give coins and instruct children to call if there is a problem or if they will be late. Even safer would be to have a group of older children followed by an adult.

Insist that youngsters use good manners, are courteous, and say "thank you" for treats received.

Review thoroughly with children all appropriate trick-or-treat safety precautions, including pedestrian/traffic safety rules.

Give children an early meal or a filling nutritious snack before they go out, so they won't be tempted to eat candy or other treats before they get home.

On the way

Selection

Stop only at houses or apartment buildings which are well-lit and/or clearly display that they are participating in trick-or-treat activities. Avoid darkened houses.

Never enter cars, homes or apartments unless an accompanying adult approves.

Walk, do not run, from house to house. Do not cross yards and lawns where unseen objects or the uneven terrain itself can present tripping hazards.

Pedestrian Safety

Walk on sidewalks, not in the street. If there are no sidewalks, walk on the left side of the road, facing traffic.

Cross busy streets at intersections or crosswalks. Do not zig-zag across the street going from door to door.

Wait for proper traffic signals when crossing streets. Look both ways before crossing. Walk, never run, across streets.

Avoid running out between parked cars.

Watch for cars entering or exiting driveways.

Avoid any horseplay, pushing or shoving, when walking close to street traffic.

If children are using bicycles, they should adjust their costumes and use bicycle pant clips or other means to avoid contact with bike spokes. Bikes should have reflectors, a headlight and a horn or bell. Follow all appropriate traffic rules.

Treats received

Insist that treats be brought home for inspection before anything is eaten.

Examine all treats carefully for unpackaged items, torn packaging, pinholes, off-color odour or questionable appearance. Wash fruits and slice them into small pieces, checking for inedible additions.

If anything is suspicious about the treats, report it to the police.

When in doubt, throw it out.

Be sure that children brush their teeth properly after eating the treats.

Preparing your home

Keep a light on so it's easy to see stairs and steps. It will also signal that you welcome trick-or-treaters.

Pick up tools, ladders, playthings, sprinklers, trash containers or other objects in the yard so children won't trip over them.

Keep family pets away from the front door so they won't frighten children. People dressed in strange costumes may also scare or irritate animals.

Wrap treats if they are loose or homemade. On homemade edibles, add your name to the package so parents will know where it came from. See ideas for nonedible treats in the next chapter.

An adult should supervise or actually do the cutting of the pumpkin, since a sharp, pointed knife is needed. If carving a pumpkin is not appropriate, or if children are very young, homemade or store-bought decals can be applied for facial features.

Jack-o'-lantern is the classic Halloween symbol. Use a flashlight in jack-o'-lanterns for a light. This is safer than a candle in case the pumpkin is accidentally knocked over, or if the flame comes in contact with decorations or costumes that could ignite.

Motorists

Slow down in residential areas.

Watch for children darting out from between parked cars.

At twilight, or later in the evening, watch for children in dark clothing.

Watch carefully when entering or exiting driveways.

Children and adults should use seat belts.

Have children get out of the car on the curb side, away from traffic.

If you are driving to a costume party, do not wear your mask while driving. Avoid wearing costumes that may constrict your arm or leg movements.

NONEDIBLE TREATS

Halloween treat nowadays usually means commercially packaged candy, chewing gum, or small boxes of fruits, nuts and seeds.

You don't need to limit your treats to sweets, though. A nonedible treat will be an interesting and welcome addition to any child's goodie bag. Collect suitable items well in advance whenever you find anything appropriate and inexpensive on sale. Let children choose from a basket of nonedible treats in addition to, or instead of, candy. Or hide the treats in little surprise boxes (save all small boxes from makeup etc.) or pumpkin-shaped, orange colored crepe or tissue paper wrappings.

No items with small parts should be given to children under age three as they may swallow them. Look for age guidelines on packages. If you prewrap nonedible treats, make a few packages for tiny toddlers, mark them and put them in a separate basket so they don't get mixed up with older children's treats.

Give only safe, desirable and non-hazardous items such as:

Plastic bugs and other spooky creatures
Novelty toys
Balloons (unblown)
Costume jewelry
Dice
Spintop
Colorful rolls of adhesive tape
Notebooks
Magnets
Instant photos of trick-or-treaters
Small balls
Coloring books
Modeling clay
Erasers
Stickers

If your pen feels creative, write and illustrate a short Halloween story, make photocopies and let your children color them (or let your children create the whole story); wrap around a pencil or a candy stick to give to trick-or-treaters.

If you are handy with crafts and have some time, consider making simple trinkets from scrap fabrics and notions for just pennies each. Here are a few such ideas:

Finger or hand puppets from felt, scrap fabrics and yarn.

Tiny stuffed animals and miniature sock dolls.

Stuffed minipumpkin.

Felt appliqué to hang on the wall.

Coin purse with Velcro strip for closure.

Crocheted spiralling worm. (Crochet a chain, then crochet 3 stitches to each chainstitch; crochet oval, flat head and add button eyes.)

Sew a little drawstring bag and add a treat inside.

Barrettes and piggytail bands.

and it was a spooky Halloween night...

TRICK OR TREAT FOR UNICEF

UNICEF, the United Nations Children's Fund, was founded in 1946 as an emergency assistance organization to help children suffering from the devastation of World War II. In 1953, its mandate was changed to emphasize the programs of long-range benefits to children of developing countries. UNICEF's efforts on behalf of the world's children have become world renowned, culminating in receiving the Nobel Peace Prize in 1965.

In 1950, a group of Pennsylvania school children collected seventeen dollars on Halloween and sent the money to UNICEF. Their initiative has since grown into a 2 million dollar a year program in both the United States and Canada that has meant better health care, nutrition, and education for the world's neediest children in over 115 countries. UNICEF's familiar orange and black fundraising box has earned its place among other traditional Halloween symbols.

In 1967, October 31st was declared National UNICEF Day in the United States by Presidential proclamation. Every Halloween, millions of Americans and Canadians of all ages are traditionally giving generously of their time, energy, and money to actively demonstrate their concern for the children of the world.

A non-profit, non-political organization, UNICEF depends entirely on voluntary contributions to finance its work. Approximately three-quarters of its income is contributed by governments. The remainder comes from many different fundraising activities but Halloween is one of the biggest.

For more than 30 years, funds raised from the traditional trick or treat collection and innumerable group benefit activities have helped to ensure a brighter future for children allover the world.

Activity brochures, posters, and promotional materials are available free of charge to help organize your school, group, or community for Halloween.

To learn more about what you can do to help UNICEF, or to start a collection campaign in your community, contact your nearest UNICEF office, or write to:

United States Committee for UNICEF
Group Programs Department
331 East 38th Street
New York, N.Y. 10016
tel: (212) 686-5522

UNICEF Canada
443 Mt. Pleasant Road
Toronto, Ontario M4S 2L8
tel. (416) 482-4444

RINA, THE PUMPKIN

JEAN-FRANÇOIS (THE BEDOUIN), ALBERT (THE SKELETON), ANGELICA (THE CAT),
SARAH (THE BUTTERFLY), AND RINA (THE CLOWN)

RINA, THE XMAS TREE
TARA, THE SNOWMAN

RINA, THE GNOME

ANGELICA (THE GHOST), ALBERT (THE ASTRONAUT), RINA (THE PUMPKIN),
MARIANE (THE BUMBLEBEE), AND SARAH (THE GIFTBOX)

HALLOWEEN AT SCHOOL

TO THE TEACHER: Make Halloween a special school-day for youngsters. Read Halloween history aloud to the class. Discuss historical, traditional and safety aspects with children. Encourage them to dress in their costumes for the day or just the afternoon. Bring a few paper bags to make quick costumes for the kids who don't have any. Take a group picture of your class with their costumes.

Children could prepare a few spooky stories in advance and read them to others. If you are planning a Halloween show or parade, make simple costumes at school as a group project. Properly stored, the costumes will last from year to year and be used by other children. Ask children to donate their own outgrown costumes to the school, since many homes don't have adequate storage space for too many costumes. Even if costumes for a simple school play are made to be disposable ones, save a few of the best to inspire others the following years.

The costumes in this book are designed without masks for safety on the street. Masks, however, are great theatrical props for school shows. To make easy no-cost masks, collect big plastic bottles with handles in advance. Rectangular-shaped containers with handles (for water, fabric softener, vinegar, dishwashing liquid, oil etc.) are ideal for this purpose. To make two masks, cut the bottle in half around sides and bottom, slitting the handle in half. Cut openings for eyes, nose and mouth. (Careful here; cutting should be done with sharp scissors or pointed knife so it's best done by an adult.) Use permanent markers to draw facial features on the mask; glue on pieces of yarn for hair, brows, mustache or beard. Each mask can be individual and different. Kids will hold the mask in front of the face by the handle. Design other masks from paper plates, posterboard and styrofoam food trays.

WHY CHILDREN LOVE TO DRESS UP

Children love to pretend, to try out roles, and to use their imagination and inventiveness. They step outside of their everyday world to scare and get scared in the safe make-believe world, where anything is possible. All this is easy and fun with costumes and accessories. Such joyous play is good for kids and it shouldn't be limited only to Halloween. Both boys and girls should be encouraged to try out any role they wish.

Dress-up play is more interesting and desirable than many toys or passive TV entertainment. Encourage your children to develop their creative imagination in making costumes from ordinary things readily available in the house.

If you have a dress-up trunk with a few basic outfits and some accessories for children, they will be ready anytime for Halloween or a masquarade party, even if you wouldn't have time to whip up another costume.

All children are creative if given half a chance and encouraged. Creativity is a wonderful and valuable attitude to keep as a permanent life-skill.

DRESS-UP TRUNK

Spark your children's imagination by starting a dress-up box or trunk to provide opportunities for creative fantasy play, and to delight them over and over again. A few simple items I made years ago, have been through dozens of plays providing different costumes for my children and their friends.

A simple mustard-colored cape (made from an old curtain with tassels around hem) served a magician, witch, fairy, king, superman and toreador, then unexpectedly turned into a beautiful wedding gown (attached underarms, leaving shoulders bare). Make a multiple-use cape reversible with one side black and one side red. Shortcut cape: Cut a large semi-circular piece of, any fabric: cut off a small half-circle piece for neck at center straight edge, trim all edges with bias tape, add button and loop or ties for closure.

A vest, that I originally made for a cowboy or sheriff, turned out to be equally handy for a rock star or punk (without shirt underneath), gangster, policeman and, with a child's mind, even a bridegroom. A white, old gown inspired an angel, baker, chef, snowman and many other roles. A yard of white, sheer nylon turned into a veil for a bride, elf or harem dancer; then it became an elegant lady's shawl tied around shoulders, then even made the child a scary ghost.

Handy items to save for costumes and props:

Old adult-size clothing, a couple of long pieces of any fabric, old sheet or curtain, lace or other sheer see-through fabric.

Old gloves, belts, hats, purses, costume jewelry, fake flowers and feathers. (Flea markets are good hunting grounds for such items.)

Fur boa. (You can make your own by sewing a long tube from fake fur, or by sewing a lining to fake fur. Or knit a lovely boa tube from long-haired mohair yarn.)

Crepe, tissue and construction paper to make feathers, flowers, hats.

Wooden and glass beads, dried pumpkin seeds, tubular macaroni, and leather thonging, strings and raffene (synthetic raffia), to make costume jewelry.

Pipe cleaners to make antennas, spectacles, headbands, jewelry.

Floral wire and other flexible wire to make jewelry, spectacles, halos, and to secure flowers and feathers in place.

Poster board, aluminium paper, paper-backed aluminium foil, disposable aluminium baking pans, poster paints, markers, vinyl etc. to create crazy hats, ponchos, etc.

Small, light lampshades can be converted into hats.

Egg cartons, styrofoam trays, clear plastic trays from cookie bags, to make helmets.

Pom-pons, tassles, ribbons, lace, buttons, corks, bottle caps, egg shaped pantyhose containers.

Frames from old sunglasses to use as spectacles. Decorate the frames with aluminium paper, paper rays, yarn, glitter etc. if desired.

Scraps of long-haired fur, or craft fur, to make mustaches, bushy eyebrows, beards. Attach brows or mustache securely and easily with rolled-up self-adhesive bandage – the kind you use on cuts (stretchy type would be best), it sticks to skin like a charm. Attach beard with elastic around head.

Onion bags to pull over head for a quick mask; a shower cap for a hat.

Narrow, round plastic bottles with a diameter up to 10 cm (4") or less (such as bottles from table syrup, freshly squeezed juice sold at fruit stands, fondue fuel – wash very well), paper tubes from paper towels, aluminium foil or plastic wrap, or round cardboard containers from powder cleansers: Cut into spiral coils to wrap around arms and legs for robot or spacesuit costumes.

Small and large scarves to wrap around head or neck, or to tie around waist as sash, or around shoulders as shawl. Large scarf could also be a cape.

Old colanders and bowls can be made into helmets and hats.

Old white sportsocks (with worn out soles) for an all-white ghost or snowman costume; cut soles away from socks leaving a strap underfoot and pull socks over shoes.

Solid styrofoam cushioning from electronic appliances etc. can be made into a helmet for a robot or spaceman.

Damaged and discarded Christmas tree ornaments and garlands to decorate a Christmas tree costume; garlands are also good for angel halos and belts.

Large icecream and margarine containers and round, large plastic bottles (such as fabric softener and chlorine bleach); wash well and let dry. Cut into crowns, hats, helmets (add strap), drums, trick-or-treat containers.

Rectangular shaped containers with a handle (such as containers for spring water, vinegar, oil, dishwashing liquid etc.); good for masks (see Halloween at School).

Leftover ribbons, cord, yarn, macrame, jute, unravelled yarn, shredded foil packages from cookies and dried fruits, can be made into wigs.

Leftover wallpaper and giftpaper, brown wrapping paper, brown grocery bags.

Old rubber ball: cut and make clown's nose, attach string to tie around head.

Large cone-shaped popcorn containers for witch and clown hats.

Inflatable broken children's pool; cut round bottom vinyl out to make a good cape.

Old clothing (such as silky or cotton underwear, pantyhose, cotton knit nightgowns and T-shirts); cut and shred for wigs.

Even small scraps of felt and other fabrics to make applique motifs for costumes.

Old sheer voile curtain to make flowers.

Old shower curtains are good for capes.

Play it safe. Remove small objects from the trunk, such as costume jewelry that may break and buttons that could be swallowed, if the trunk will be used by children under age three.

TRICK-OR-TREAT BAGS

You could, of course, let the child grab an old, crumpled plastic bag but why not make it something special? Try matching the treat bag with the costume; it will make a great prop.

Give a little old lady an old purse, Little Red Riding Hood a basket and a doctor a "medicine bag".

Or turn a costume prop into treatbag by making an opening in drummer boy's "drum" for goodies and using Robin Hood's hunting bag as a natural goodie bag, too.

For some other costumes, consider making the goodie bag from the same material as the costume and trims.

Or sew a large tote from any suitable fabric and turn it into a family heirloom by sewing appliqués of Halloween symbols on it. Cut a piece of fabric (40 cm x 110 cm, or 16" x 43", or slightly smaller for preschoolers), cut appliqués from bright orange, black, and white fabrics (jack-o'-lanterns, witches, black cats, ghosts, skeletons, etc.) and sew them in place with satinstitch (wide, short zigzag). Fold the fabric in half and stitch side seams so that the fold is at the bottom. Sew a casing around upper edge, leaving an opening for cord. Insert a long cord through opening and tie securely, adjusting to desired length.

Hands might be full of other things, such as flashlight, Unicef-box or mittens. To free hands for doorbells or holding bigger child's or adult's hand, the bag can be designed with a longer cord so that it can be slipped overhead to hang on the opposite hip.

The bag should not be so long that it would drag on the ground, nor of heavy material, since the goodies will make it a lot heavier to carry along.

Other funny ideas for a treatbag: pillowcase, garbage bag, an old hat turned upside down with ribbon for handle, plant basket, plastic containers covered with self-adhesive vinyl and appropriately decorated with Halloween decals, with strong ribbon attached for handle.

Turn a milk container into a lantern. Cover it with yellow self-adhesive vinyl, decorate with strips of black vinyl, cut a hole in top for goodies. Make a handle from ribbon or cord inserted through holes punched near top.

Empty small containers into a larger plastic bag carried by an adult, so they won't become too full or heavy for children.

An inexpensive and quite nice container for goodies is a pumpkin-shaped plastic container commonly available during Halloween.

MAKEUP

Homemade makeup recipe

Make a batch of this non-toxic nature's makeup that is easy to wash away.

Two tablespoons cornstarch
One tablespoon solid shortening

Mix ingredients well. Makes enough white makeup for one face. Store in a small, closed jar if not used immediately. Double the recipe for two kids or if different colors are required. Divide white makeup into small portions on a piece of wax paper, and color the portions with food coloring. A package of food coloring at your supermarket contains yellow, red, green and blue in small, separate bottles. By mixing them as mentioned on the package, you can also make orange, brown and purple.

Apply makeup on skin by using fingers or cosmetic sponge, and avoid getting it near eyes. After applying the makeup, pat skin with cotton balls and talcum or baby powder for a better, longer-lasting result. Supplement with regular makeup, such as lipstick, blusher, eye shadows and brow pencils.

Homemade glue for facial decals

This nature's glue is safe for face and easy to make. Cook one large potato in its skin until tender. Let cool. Cut in two and use the cut surfaces as a glue. Cut small decals (stars, moon, hearts, flowers, terrible scars) from bright colored tissue paper (because it is sufficiently absorbent), rub the decals with cooked potato, and stick on clean, dry cheeks and forehead. Potato glue is equally handy to stick glitter on the face.

Potato glue decals peel off easily and are suitable for short time use only.

WIGS

Wigs are wonderful disguises and any child would love to have one. They are optional costume accessories depending on your available time and budget. A wig can be made so warm that it will replace a hat in a cold climate. When using a wig, brush child's own hair neatly upward and hold it in place with elastic band, bobby pins, or hair net, so it will not show under the wig.

Here are a few easy ideas for different wigs. Each one can be made in an evening or less. Older children can help in designing and making the wigs as a group project. Look at dolls; many of them have lovely yarn hair to inspire you in creating similar wigs.

Short-haired wig with sewing machine

Cut basecap from lightweight cotton-type fabric with pattern W-6. Try using the same colored fabric as the yarn to make it less visible. Do not sew the cap seams yet. Wind craft yarn around milk container (or a strip of cardboard of desired length), with strands side by side but not overlapping. Stick strands together with masking tape. Pull the milk container or cardboard out. Machine stitch yarn strands together across the center, and pull masking tape off. Stitch to basecap along first stitching line, cutting the prepared yarn strip into

shorter sections as needed. Fold yarn ends out of way for the second stitching line. Prepare additional yarn hair the same way and stitch it in place to basecap, covering it all over. Cut the loops, and brush strands open for silky or curly hair depending on yarn type and length. After all the hair is sewn in place, stitch basecap side slits closed. Stitch sretched elastic around edge, turn elasticized edge under and stitch in place.

Jute wig for troll

Use the same method to make a wig from jute. Brush strands open, backcomb them and spray with hairspray.

Wig with latch hook

Cut the basecap from needlepoint canvas, or soft rug canvas, with large mesh. You might even find mesh fabrics designed for curtains or garments suitable, if they have large enough mesh and enough stiffness. Stitch side slits closed. Stitch stretched elastic around edges. Cut thick craft yarn into pieces twice as long as the desired finished length of hair (adding 2.5cm/1" for the knot). Work cut yarn into cap's mesh, pulling yarn ends through folded center loop, with a handy, inexpensive latch hook generally used for rugs. (Even crochet hook works but will take longer.) Depending on yarn thickness and mesh size, hook only every second or third hole. Tighten knots, trim ends to desired length.

Wig for African Dancer

Use either method mentioned before, but be sure to use yarn with tightly twisted strands.

When the wig is finished, split strands with fingers for curly hair.

Long wig

Cut basecap as before. Depending on the thickness of the yarn, cut about 200-300 strands, about one metre or yard long each.

Lay the strands parallel on the table or floor; tape them together with masking tape on both sides, leaving center free. Machine or handstitch the yarn strands securely in place to basecap from center front to neck. Turn all yarn out of way, and stitch side slits of basecap closed. Stitch elastic around all edges, turn elasticized edge under and stitch in place.

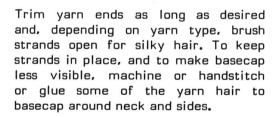

Trim yarn ends as long as desired and, depending on yarn type, brush strands open for silky hair. To keep strands in place, and to make basecap less visible, machine or handstitch or glue some of the yarn hair to basecap around neck and sides.

Make braids or piggytails or leave the hair open.

WORKING WITH CREPE PAPER

Available in regular and heavy-duty strength in a wide range of brilliant colors, crepe paper is excellent for flowers, feathers, hats, other accessories, and even for some costumes. It is inexpensive, strong, flameproof, and stretchable. Seams can be sewn by hand using a darning needle, yarn and long stitches. Or seams can simply be taped together with masking tape or attached with craft or fabric glue. (Regular transparent cellophane tape doesn't stick well to crepe paper, regular white household glue puckers it.) Or bond seams together with fusible web instead of gluing them. Cut crepe paper so that the stretchy length becomes width, then the paper won't stretch out of shape.

Flowers

Here are just a few possibilites. Working with crepe paper will inspire you to create many more. Use roses and daisies for Bride; attach a few flowers together with floral wire and tape, then attach them to an elastic hairband; make a bouquet by attaching many flowers together at stems with floral wire and tape. Use exotic flowers in African Dancer's hair and for Hawaiian Hula Dancer's lei and in hair; attach flowers to long ribbons with floral wire and tape; tie around neck and head. Make petal flowers, or easy sweet peas, for Elf.

Daisy: For the center, make a small ball from facial tissue; wrap a 10cm/4" square of yellow crepe paper around it, twisting the ends into a long stem. Fold a strip of white crepe paper (20x15cm or 8x6") in half lengthwise crossgrain. Cut narrow strips (5cm/2" long) into folded edge. Wrap cut edges around the stem with glue, floral tape or wire. Spread petals in all directions.

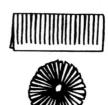

Exotic flower: You need three different, bright colors of crepe paper. For each flower, cut three strips 10x15cm (4x6"), one of each color, place them on top of each other (royal blue under, purple in the middle, yellow on top). Fold the layers in half lengthwise crossgrain. Insert thin floral wire between center fold. Cut upper edges into narrow strips. Bend wire ends down and twist them together, while pushing folded edge of crepe paper layers tightly toward center.

Petal flower: For each flower, make white or yellow center (see daisy). Or create different center stamens from pipe cleaners, shredded construction paper, or tightly rolled-up strips of either crepe paper or paper-backed aluminium foil. Cut six petals from green crepe paper, arrange them around the center, gathering each base a bit; wrap tightly with floral wire or tape.

Rose: Take a strip of red crepe paper (20x15cm or 8x6"), fold it in half lengthwise crossgrain. Roll up the cut edges tightly with glue,

string or floral wire. Stretch folded
edges; press outer edges downward.

Sweet pea: Made in different sizes
and colors, this lovely flower is
suitable for any purpose. For each
flower, cut three circles from crepe
paper (or tissue paper, tulle, chiffon,
or vinyl), with a diameter of 5-
8cm (2-3"). Place circles on top
of each other; fold them in half.
Insert thin floral wire between center
fold. Bend wire ends down and twist
them together, while pushing folded
edge tightly toward center. Spread
and stretch petals.

Grass skirt, peplum skirt and decorations for African Dancer

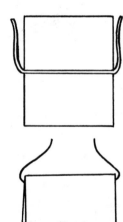

To make a small size grass skirt
for African Dancer and Hawaiian
Hula Dancer, cut three sheets
(66cm/26" long x 51cm/20" wide)
of green crepe paper, and fold them
lengthwise crossgrain. Open the
fold, and glue the sheets together
along the center fold. Refold the
sheets to make six layers. Glue
a strong, 76cm/30" long ribbon
between the center fold, leaving
ends extending for ties. Cut all
layers into 1.3cm/½" wide, 20cm/8"
long strips from hem upward.

The width of a crepe paper roll
is not wide enough to fold in two
for the skirt length of medium and
large sizes, so you have to cut the
sheets separately and glue them
together at waist. For medium size,
cut six sheets 71cm/28" long and
36cm/14" wide each (the non-stretchy

width becomes the length of the finished skirt). For large size, cut six sheets 76cm/30" long and 41cm/16" wide each. Glue long sides of the six sheets together at waist while gluing a strong, 100cm/40" long ribbon between the layers, with ends extending on each side for ties. Cut all six sheets into 1.3cm/½" wide, 31cm/12" long (or 36cm/14" long for large size) strips from hem upward. Tie the skirt around waist. When making the peplum skirt, cut the six layers into large petals instead of strips.

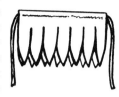

To make decorations for African Dancer's ankles and wrists, cut two sheets of red crepe paper (38x31cm/15x12"), fold in half lengthwise crossgrain, glue the layers together at center fold with long ribbon between the layers. Refold, and cut lower edges into strips like skirt; tie the decorations (twice) around wrists and ankles. For hair, make a huge exotic flower from red crepe paper (page 37); attach it to an elastic hairband.

Indian tribesman headdress

Cut about 30 feathers from white, heavy-duty crepe paper (or from white construction paper), about 25cm/10" long each, tapering upper ends into narrow points. To make headband, an 84cm/33" long, 8cm/3" wide, strip is cut from green felt (or other suitable fabric); iron it in half lengthwise. Gather the base of each feather to stiffen it, and glue the feathers side-by-side between

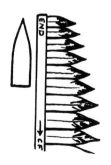

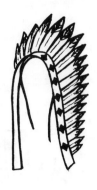

the folded felt strip. Trim feathers at each end of felt strip a bit shorter and narrower. Paint feather tips with black marker. Cut a piece of strong twill tape, or other suitable ribbon, 76x2.5cm (30x1"). Placing felt band center at twill tape center, glue or sew them together at the forehead for 25cm/10", leaving twill tape ends extending for tying behind the head. The ends of the green felt strip with feathers trail down on each side. Cut diamonds from orange or red felt, and glue them on top of green felt band for decoration (or use wide rickrack trim).

Pom-pon for Cheerleader

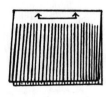

Cut four sheets (64x56cm or 25x22") of crepe paper, two blue and two white; fold each sheet in half lengthwise crossgrain. Open the folded sheets and place them on top of each other, alternating the colors. Glue the layers together at the center fold. Refold the sheets to make eight layers. Cut the layers into 1.3cm/½" wide, 20cm/8" long strips from lower edge upward. To make handle, tie ends of a 51cm/20" piece of strong rope together; glue folded edge of crepe papers around knotted ends of rope, rolling it tightly in place. Tie strong cord, ribbon or wire around the base to cover folded crepe paper edge. (You could also attach the rope to the top of a lightweight plastic bottle with wide opening; glue shredded crepe paper layers around the bottle to hide it from sight, and leave top open for treats.)

OTHER ACCESSORIES

Balloon-mold papier-mâché helmet for Octopus

The helmet is made by pasting paper or fabric strips over an inflated balloon. Although this takes some time to make, it is easy and fun, and the kids find the process fascinating. Let them watch and help. The result is a lightweight, smooth, balloon-shaped helmet, that can be cut and painted. Once you master the technique, you can use it for other craft projects, too.

To make a thin, creamy paste, mix one part of powdered wallpaper paste with 10 parts of water. Or mix white household glue with an equal amount of water. For fireproofing, add one teaspoon of sodium phosphate (from drugstore) to each cup of paste. Blow up a round balloon until its circumference is a bit larger than child's head, or about 62cm (24½"); tie with string. Tape the balloon securely on top of a small, heavy bowl or mug. When preparing strips (from tissue paper, newspaper or gauze fabric), don't cut them, tear them against a straightedge. Rough edges will mesh for a smooth surface.

Brush the balloon with prepared paste. Dip the paper or fabric strips in water and cover the balloon with them, overlapping each strip slightly. (Cover only about upper 2/3 of the balloon since you will be trimming lower part off.) Brush the balloon again with paste, and then place another layer of wet paper or fabric strips on top of the first layer, overlapping the strips. Repeat alternate layers of paste and paper/fabric strips, until you have at least six layers of paper or four layers of fabric. Smooth out any wrinkles.

Let dry overnight until hard. Let air out of balloon; the balloon comes out easily and can be discarded. Cut the helmet as desired to cover the child's head and ears. Punch small holes in each side and add elastic chinstrap. Paint the helmet with acrylic or poster paints or any water-base paint. For water-proofing and durability, spray with clear vinyl sealer or brush with lacquer.

Using different paste, papers or fabrics gives different results. Tissue paper is smooth and featherweight especially when wallpaper paste is used. If you use paper or fabric strips of desired color, you don't even need to paint the finished helmet.

Clown nose

If you don't have plastic nose for clown, or an old, red rubber ball which can be cut and tied in place with string, here are other easy ways to create that round, big nose.

Cut one egg cup from an egg container (styrofoam container is best since it is round and smooth); paint red with acrylic or poster paints; stick on nose with rolled-up bandage.

If you have a red plastic egg, stick half of it on nose. Or make the nose from real eggshell. Take unbroken half of an eggshell, wash it well; brush it with white, non-toxic household glue, then cover it with a few layers of wet, narrow strips of red tissue paper. Let dry. [You can speed drying with hair dryer.] Stick it on nose with rolled-up bandage (stretchy type works best).

Costume jewelry

Costume jewelry is fun and easy to make from metal paper, metallic ribbons, flexible wire, raffene, leather thongings, aluminium foil and paper-backed aluminium foil, wooden or glass beads and buttons, etc. Here are just a few possibilites. You and the children are bound to invent many others while working with inspiring craft materials.

Wind flexible wire around wooden coloring crayon that has a smooth, rounded surface. It makes a lovely, spiralling necklace or bracelet. You can also stretch the finished spiral a bit, and press it flat under a heavy pot.

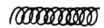

Make wire spiralling, cut it into 2.5cm/1" pieces, then string spiral pieces alternately with wooden beads for a necklace.

Knot macrame cord, ribbon, raffene or leather thonging between glass or wooden beads, or pretty buttons.

Take a long strip of 8cm/3" wide aluminium foil, roll it lightly lengthwise and twist; turn into necklace (ends can be attached with string) and press flat under a heavy pot. You might like to glue a few diamonds from blue or red paper-backed aluminium foil on the flattened necklace.

Take two long strips (2.5cm/1" wide each) of paper-backed aluminium foil in contrasting colors, or use one strip aluminium paper and one strip of construction paper; glue each strip in half lengthwise. Fold strips alternately on top of each other into 1.3cm/½" squares. You end up with a two-colored, flexible, three-dimensional band that makes a pretty necklace. Attach ends with string.

Cut two collars from yellow construction paper, or from yellow paper-backed aluminium foil (make a pattern first to fit around child's neck). Glue papers together. Cut large diamonds from blue paper-backed aluminium foil, and glue them around the collar. Glue smaller yellow or green diamonds on top of blue ones. Glue some glitter on the top. Tie ends with string.

Drum and drumsticks

This drum doubles as a trick-or-treat collector, made from a large, round cardboard or plastic container (such as ice cream container or bleach bottle; cut the top off the bottle). Glue bright red fabric or self-adhesive vinyl around the container. From strong, flexible yellow vinyl (or double-layered vinyl) or synthetic leather, cut two circles with a diameter 5cm/2" larger than the container, one for top and one for the bottom. Cut a hole in the middle of top circle for treats. Cut small holes all around edges of both top and bottom circles. Insert strong, yellow cord through edge holes, crisscrossing between top and bottom and tie them together. Attach a long strap securely to drum for carrying around the neck.

Drumsticks: Push knitting needles or thin wooden sticks tightly into large wooden beads (wrap ends with masking tape if bead hole is too large). Wrap the sticks tightly with paper strips until desired thickness, then wrap them with decorative, adhesive tape or self-adhesive vinyl.

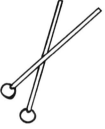

Egg container helmet

You will need seven cardboard egg containers. (Don't use styrofoam containers; spray paint will melt or bubble them.) Cut off all top sections and discard them. Cut off the last two cups from each of five bottom sections, so that they will have two rows of five egg cups.

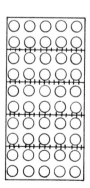

Using yarn and darning needle, sew these five sections side-by-side into a row; this will go around the head to cover the back and sides. To make the top, sew the two remaining sections together side-by-side, cut off ends and then all four corner cups.

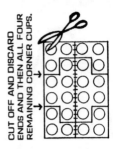

Sew the prepared back and side-section row to the top section around back and sides, so that front remains open for face. Spray paint the outside of helmet silver. Add elastic chinstrap. (Spray painting is best done outdoors; protect driveway or grass with newspapers, wear old clothes and plastic gloves. Or put the helmet into a large transparent plastic bag; tie top with rubber band. Slip your hand through top opening and spray the helmet inside the bag.)

Eyebrows, beards and mustaches

Use scraps of real or fake fur or long-haired craft fur, and cut to any shape you need. Attach eyebrows or mustache securely with rolled-up bandage (stretchy type works best). Secure beard in place with elastic strap around head.

Beards can also be made from craft yarn. Cut a beard-shaped piece in any suitable fabric. Starting from bottom up, cover the fabric entirely with pieces of craft yarn (gluing only upper ends to fabric and overlapping successive layers). Let dry thoroughly; punch holes at sides for elastic band. Brush each yarn strand open for hairy look.

When making yarn beard for gnome, wind yarn around a piece of cardboard or milk container, then stick masking tape across yarn strands to hold them together as cardboard or container is pulled out. Stitch a long piece of twill tape or any suitable

ribbon across the yarn strands, leaving
ends extending on each side for
ties. Pull the masking tape off.
Fold all yarn loops to one side; cut
the loops open. Tie the beard in
place.

Mustaches can also be cut into any
shape from felt or construction
paper. Or with craft yarn, tie a
bunch of 25cm/10" long strands
together in the middle; brush strands
open into silky hair; trim the mustache
to your liking. (Stiffen with hair
spray, if necessary.)

Stick the mustache under nose with
rolled-up, self-adhesive, stretchy
bandage.

Fringes

Fringes are easy to make from craft
yarn for a handsome edge of Mexican
poncho, or for Drummer's epaulet
decorations.

Wind yarn around a piece of cardboard
(20cm/8" long); cut strands along
one edge, divide them into groups
of 3 strands, and fold each group
in half.

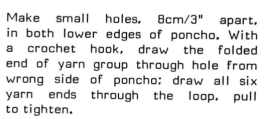

Make small holes, 8cm/3" apart,
in both lower edges of poncho. With
a crochet hook, draw the folded
end of yarn group through hole from
wrong side of poncho; draw all six
yarn ends through the loop, pull
to tighten.

Finished length of fringe is about
17.5cm/7". Change cardboard size
if different length is needed.

Pom-pons from craft yarn

Use these pom-pons for bunny, clown, gnome hat and Santa Claus.

Cut a piece of cardboard 5x15cm (2x6"). Wind yarn around cardboard the desired fullness. Slip a 38cm/15" long piece of strong yarn or cord through lower edge, tie tightly and leave ends extending. Cut through upper edge of folded yarn.

Roll the pom-pon in your hands to spread the strands evenly. Insert long yarn ends through darning needle to tack the pom-pon in place.

Whiskers

Make whiskers from stiff thread, dental floss, or cord (paint with markers and stiffen with hairspray, if necessary), or from pipe cleaners, raffene (synthetic raffia) or broom straws.

Tie a few long strands together in the middle, and stick them under nose with rolled-up self-adhesive bandage (stretchy type works best).

Or draw the whiskers directly on cheeks with a brow pencil.

COSTUMES

It is hard to say what's more fun for kids, all that candy or dressing-up. Probably it is the unbeatable combination of the two.

Homemade costumes are more original and more fun than store-bought plastic versions and masks. Include your children in choosing and creating an original Halloween costume. Don't be surprised if your sweet little girl dreams of becoming a ghost or witch, or if your cool, self-assured son decides to become an angel.

Role playing is good for kids and it's just a game. In fact, your kids may want to be so many different characters that it's a pity Halloween is only once a year. Be sure to take snapshots of your kids in their costumes.

Materials

Use any suitable material you may have on hand, such as old sheets, tablecloths, bedspreads, curtains, old clothing. Fabrics should be lightweight and light-colored, or trimmed with reflective tapes or decals. Try finding flameproof fabrics by checking the tag on the fabric bolt. Generally speaking, manmade fabrics are more flameproof than natural fibers. See chapter "Make Halloween Safe - Costumes" for directions on how to flameproof homemade costumes.

Shop for suitable fabrics at factory outlets, discount stores and sales. Drapery and furniture upholtery sections of big discount fabric stores are good places for bargains. Bolt ends and fabrics with any irregularities are inexpensive and just right for costumes. The same goes for fancy, metallic and other unusual, synthetic fabrics off-season; they will make lovely costumes.

Crepe paper is suitable for many accessories and even some costumes. See chapter "Working with crepe paper".

Enlarging miniature patterns

The miniature patterns in this book are drawn in two different manners. The simplest patterns (from A to S) are drawn to <u>scale</u>; the remaining patterns (from T to Z) are drawn onto <u>grids.</u>

To enlarge scale patterns, use any paper (brown paper or even newspaper is fine), or enlarge the pattern directly onto fabric if you are an experienced seamstress. The measurements to enlarge scale patterns are given first in metric, and then in imperial system, first mentioning size small, then size medium (in brackets), and then size large. If you choose to use imperial measurements, ignore the metric ones, or the other way around. If desired, mark the necessary measurements first with highlight pen for the size you are enlarging. Draw the full-size pattern by measuring the distances between all points as mentioned in the miniature pattern, and then connect the points with straight or curved lines, as shown. Starting point is marked X. When bodice front and back are drawn together, and the pattern shows two necklines, the lower one is for front.

To enlarge grid patterns, draw a grid of 2.5cm/1" squares on a sheet of paper, or tape tracing or wax paper on cardboard cutting board, or macrame board, marked with grid. Enlarge the miniature pattern to full-size grid by marking all corners, and then connect them dot-to-dot with straight or curved lines as shown.

Reusable vinyl sheets with ready-made grid are also available commercially.

Fabric requirements and seam allowances

Fabric requirements are mentioned for the most likely (or most convenient) width of fabric, <u>always mentioning first the length, then the width.</u> If you use fabric of different width, measure from miniature or enlarged pattern to find out how much fabric is needed; or take this book or the enlarged pattern with you to the store. Patterns <u>include</u> seam allowances of 1cm (3/8"), and hem allowances of 2.5-5cm (1-2").

Since the costume patterns are drawn in three sizes, small(medium)large, and in both metric and imperial measurements, you have to learn to correctly interpret my measurement lists.

Example: For pattern A, the fabric required for long gown is listed as following: 125(190)210cm x 115(140)140cm, or 50(75)82" x 45(55)55". This means, that if you are using imperial measurements and choose size medium, you would need a 75" long piece of 55" wide fabric.

Fabrics are suggested for some costumes. Be inventive and use fabrics and colors of your choice. Read the pattern instructions and costume description through, jotting down what fabric and notions you need to make up the costume.

Simple directions

My directions for completing each garment are short and simple on purpose. Long and complicated directions tend to be discouraging and make the job sound more difficult than it really is. Naturally you need to know basic sewing techniques before using patterns with such short directions. Plan the cutting layout for all pieces prior to cutting the fabric.

Metric and imperial measurements

Both measuring systems are provided. The measurements may differ slightly and, for practical purposes, show rounded figures, but the difference is irrelevant and you may confidently choose to use either system.

Pattern sizes

This book contains patterns for children in sizes fitting children three to twelve years old. The majority of costumes are loose-fitting, and the size is easy to enlarge or reduce for your child. If you need to enlarge any pattern size, cut the pattern apart vertically and horizontally, and spread the pieces apart until desired size is achieved; tape a piece of paper underneath to bridge the separated pieces together. When you need to reduce the pattern size, pleat the pattern vertically and/or horizontally at several points until desired size is achieved. Tape the pleats in place or use pins, so you can easily remove them later and use the larger size when your child will grow into it.

The patterns are drawn for the following three sizes:

Children sizes	Small	Medium	Large
Years	3-4	6-8	10-12
Height cm	100-110	120-135	145-155
Height inches	39½-43½	47-53	57-61
Chest cm	53-58	64-68	73-76
Chest inches	21-23	25-27	29-30

Marks used in patterns

▬▬▬▬▬▬	Cutting line
	Place the pattern on fold of fabric. DO NOT CUT ON THIS LINE. (Fold on lengthwise straight grain.)
▬ ▬ ▬ ▬ ▬ ▬	Gather (by sewing two rows of long stitches close to each other and pulling the bobbin threads to distribute fullness evenly in gathers).
◄───────►	Place on straight lengthwise grain.
• • • • • • • •	Foldline
1, 2,	Match same numbers when sewing.
CF CB	Center front Center back
F B	Front Back
S M L	Small Medium Large
X	Starting point

1. AFRICAN DANCER

Brown bodysuit (pattern U) and tights, or pants and sweatshirt.

Red decorations for hair, wrists and ankles, and green grass skirt are made from crepe paper (see pages 38-39).

(Optional black wig, see page 35.) Face: Brown makeup, red and blue markings. Costume jewelry, or tie colorful wooden or glass beads to ribbons or leather thonging. Sash: Tie colorful scarf around waist. Decorate tote bag with shredded red and green crepe paper.

2. ANGEL

Roll a long strip of aluminium foil, twist it into a rope (or wind Christmas tree garland tightly around flexible metal wire), then form into a halo. Affix the halo with bobby pins or elastic chinstrap.

Sew white or pastel-colored robe from pattern A, decorate it with metallic gold braid and also tie braid around waist. White poster board wings from pattern T-1; armstraps. Glue glitter on wings.

Sew a tote from leftover robe fabric and decorate it with metallic braid and glitter as for robe and wings.

3. ANIMAL COSTUMES (BUNNY, CAT, MOUSE)

Lined hood from pattern W-1; coveralls from pattern D with zippered front; spats from pattern Y-1; mittens from pattern X-1. Appropriate ears and tails. Suggested fabrics for animal costumes, hoods, mittens and spats: Fake fur (old car seat covers are great), velour, sweatsuit fabric with fleecy side up.

Bunny has white costume and accessories; huge pom-pons for buttons and tail (page 48). Cut two long front teeth from white plastic or wax container (leave the teeth attached along upper edge) and affix them over upper lip with rolled-up bandage. Draw black nose tip. Make white whiskers from pipe cleaners, raffene or stiff thread; tie a few strands together in the middle, and affix the whiskers under nose with rolled-up self-adhesive, stretchy bandage.

Cat's costume and accessories are made from black fabric; long stuffed tail. Use makeup to draw slanted eyes and black nose tip. Black whiskers (see bunny).

Mouse has gray costume and accessories, large round ears with black or pink fronts, and stuffed long tail. Draw black circles around eyes and black nose tip. Black or gray whiskers.

4. ASTRONAUT

Make a helmet from large, round plastic container or poster board (cover with aluminium paper or spray paint silver); glue on corks and bottle caps for knobs, and attach a long pipe cleaner for antenna.

Silver or blue nylon coveralls from pattern D. Appliqué stiff fabric or paint cardboard to make blue Nasa badge with white lettering.

Cut four round shields from disposable aluminium baking pans, decorate them with permanent markers and baste on shoulders and knees. For cold climates, make a pair of mittens with pattern X-1, from the same fabric as the costume, with flannelette lining.

5. BALLERINA

Tie twisted scarf or blue and pink satin ribbons around head.

White or pink bodysuit (pattern U) and tights. Electric blue (or your child's favorite color) tutu from pattern V-1 decorated with lace and sequins. Blue slippers without soles (pattern V-2), are pulled over sneakers and tied around ankles with long ribbons.

(Easy tutu pattern also makes a lovely sundress in cotton knit.)

6. BAT

Brown, lined hood with ears, and drawstring ribknit neckband from pattern W-1. Brown sweatsuit from pattern C (or use any brown pants and top).

Wings (pattern T-2) with armstraps are made from black poster board.

Draw black circles around eyes and spread brown makeup on face.

Appliqué or glue a scary black bat on a tote bag.

7. BEDOUIN

White headwear: Use a large scarf or towel, or a small tablecloth; put it over head so that front comes down to eyebrows, and sides and back fall below shoulders. Keep the headwear securely in place with elastic hairband; cover headband with rope or twisted scarf.

Bushy eyebrows and black mustache are made from fur or craft yarn (see page 46). Affix them to skin with rolled-up self-adhesive, stretchy bandages.

Striped or white djellaba robe from pattern E, with front slit. (Optional: Tie a rope around waist.)

8. BELLY DANCER

Skintone bodysuit (pattern U), and tights.

Veil: Use an old sheer tablecloth or curtain, or a large piece of any transparent, lightweight fabric over head; keep it in place with elastic headband and safety pins.

Lots of costume jewelry around neck, waist and wrists (see page 43).

Make the costume from fancy, sheer fabric; baggy pants from pattern M-1 and top with lace trim from pattern M-2.

9. BRIDE

White veil: Fold a large piece of sheer, lightweight fabric (such as tulle, voile, lace, nylon, chiffon, net) in half, so that upper half is shorter. Slip elastic hairband between the two layers, gather folded edge and tack it securely to elastic hairband; cover with flowers (page 36). White gown from pattern A, with lace trim around neck and sleeve ends. Satin ribbons tied around arms and under bust. Flower bouquet from crepe paper (page 36) attached to ribbon under bust. Paint on a pretty face.

Decorate a white drawstring bag with lace, ribbons and fake flowers.

10. BUMBLEBEE

Black balaclava helmet from pattern W-2; tack black pipe cleaners on top for antennas.

Wings with armstraps from yellow poster board (pattern T-3).

Yellow pullover neck ruffle (pattern F-2) from fake fur, velvet, velour or sweatshirt fabric (fleecy side out); elastic around neck.

Costume (pattern F-1) from yellow/black striped fabric (same fabrics as for neck ruffle; striped, or 10cm/4" wide strips of two colors sewn together). Zippered front. Black or yellow mittens (pattern X-1).

11. BUTTERFLY

Attach long pipe cleaners on top of black balaclava helmet (pattern W-2) for antennas.

Costume is made from two sheets of poster board (pattern T-5). Paint or glue bright designs in many colors on each set of wings and on the butterfly body in the middle. For ideas, find beautiful butterfly designs in children's illustrated books.

Punch holes at waist and shoulders, through both sets of wings, and tie them together with ribbons.

12. CHEERLEADER

Decorate hair with ribbons or twisted elastic hairband, or twist blue and white (or favorite colored) scarves together and tie them around head.

White turtleneck from pattern I. Cut a huge monogram from blue felt and tack it temporarily on the front. Blue miniskirt from pattern H-1, elasticized waist. White stretchy panties from pattern H-2.

Skintone tights, white kneehigh socks and white sneakers.

White and blue crepe paper pom-pon (page 40). Pom-pon can also be made around a wide-mouthed plastic bottle, so that bottle's opening can be used to collect candy.

13. CHEF

Hat: Cut a strip of white poster board (about 8x56cm or 3x22"); glue or sew into a circle. Pleat a large circle (diameter 66cm/26") of white, stiff fabric or crepe paper all around edges, and sew or staple it under band. (Paper bag under crown will hold hat up if the fabric is not stiff enough.) Add elastic chinstrap. White coveralls from pattern D. White scarf tied around neck. Add a bit of white makeup on nose and cheeks for "flour spots".

14. CLOWNS

Use many varied, bright colors for costume and accessories. Cone-shaped hat from poster board (pattern W3), pom-pon on top (page 48), elastic chinstrap; glue craft yarn hair around hat's lower edge.

Face painted white, huge red mouth, raised brows, black lines above and below eyes. Nose is one section from egg carton painted red (cut adequate space for nostrils); stick it on nose with rolled-up self-adhesive, stretchy bandage.

Neck ruffle from fabric or crepe paper (small 18x140cm or 7x55"; medium/large 25x180cm or 10x71"). Baste long stitches in upper edge with strong thread, forming large gathers; tie at back.

Particolored (i.e. having different colors in different parts) coveralls from pattern D; self-ruffled wrists and ankles. Pom-pon buttons (page 48).

Second clown has a basecap (pattern W-6); sew craft yarn hair around lower edge. Clowny face paint. Huge bow under chin: Cut it from cardboard, paint with bright polkadots, or glue fabric on it; elastic strap around neck. Baggy pants (pattern M-1); plastic tube or stiff wire through waist casing. Use real suspenders to hold pants up, or cut suspenders from bright elastic band, criss-cross at back and sew to pants' waist with buttons.

15. COWBOY

Attach cord chinstrap to an old hat. (If you don't have a suitable hat, make one from a paperbag and cardboard: Paperbag should fit snugly on head upside down; shorten to desired length; cut a large oval from brown cardboard for brim; cut an oval hole in the middle, slightly smaller than child's head; clip bag's lower edge and glue the clipped edge under brim.)

Wear a plaid shirt. (Use mom's or dad's if necessary; baste sleeves temporarily shorter at midarms. Tie a scarf around neck. Vest from pattern J. Cardboard spats from pattern Y-3, tied at back, decorated with markers.

Gun case (pattern Z-1) with toy gun, attached to belt. (Sheriff: Add a cardboard star, covered with aluminium foil.)

16. DEVIL

Red hood (pattern W-1), with horns (horns from pattern W-18). Facial makeup: red paint on face, black around lips and eyes.

Red cape from pattern K. Orange and yellow flame motifs appliquéd, glued or painted on fabric. Tail is made from red braided cord glued between two red cardboard triangle tips; tied at back around waist.

17. DRUMMER

Red poster board hat with black brim and feather (pattern W-4). Thick, braided chinstrap from yellow craft yarn, 61 cm/24" long; leave one end hanging as a tassel.

Black blouse (pattern B). Cut epaulets from red poster board; trim with gold metallic braid or yellow ribbons; attach yarn fringes to outer ends (page 47); tack the epaulets on shoulders. Decorate sleeve ends and front with ribbons, like epaulets.

Drum made from large plastic container collects treats (see page 44 to make drum and drumsticks).

18. ELF

Elves are tiny, airy nature spirits who love carefree dancing in forests and meadows.

Skintone or green bodysuit (pattern U) and tights. Some elves have tiny wings; they can be made from green tulle or crepe paper with pattern T-3. Elastic ribbon covered with floral tape for hairband, green and yellow sweet peas from crepe paper (page 36). Attach these to hairband, to ribbons hanging from the band, and to ribbons around neck and wrists. Peplum skirt made from green crepe paper (see page 38); glue yellow sequins to peplum tips and wings with clear nail varnish or craft adhesive.

19. FAIRY

Cone-shaped hat (pattern W-3) from blue poster board; attach sheer chiffon scarf to the back seam as shown; add elastic chinstrap. Blue sheer robe from pattern A; decorate bodice and sleeves with gold metallic ribbons.

Wings made from blue fabric or crepe paper (pattern T-4). Cut three large golden stars from metallic paper, glue one on cardboard and attach it to hat's front; glue the remaining two stars together to cover the tip of a long stick for a magic wand.

Glue glitter on hat, scarf, stars and wings.

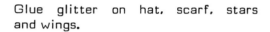

20. FLOWER

Harvest-time flower with orange petals and leaves. Headwear (pattern W-5) from orange poster board; elastic strap around back of head holds it in place. Paint a pretty face.

Brown gown from pattern A. Appliqué, paint, glue, or sew on orange stem and leaves (of felt or other suitable fabric, or poster board) from hem to neck prior to sewing the seams.

Sew a tote bag from leftover gown fabric; appliqué, paint or glue flower and leaves on it to repeat the costume design in miniature.

21. FRANKENSTEIN

Black square cardboard box (or paint any box black) to fit snugly over head; leave back and sides longer and shred front into "hair". Punch holes in each side and attach elastic chinstrap.

Paint face green with makeup; black thick eyebrows and black bleeding lines around lips, lipstick and brow pencil scars.

Sew a black or green cape with drawstring from pattern K.

22. FRIAR

Brown, hooded shoulder cloak from pattern L.

Long brown robe from pattern A.

Belt: Tie rope around waist.

Cut a cross from cardboard and cover it with metallic paper. Punch a hole for chain or cord and hang around neck.

The robe is large enough to fit over warm clothing. If it's cold outside, also make brown balaclava helmet (pattern W-2), and brown gloves or mittens (pattern X).

23. GALAXY KID

Helmet from egg cartons shown on page 45, spray-painted silver, elastic chinstrap. Draw blue rays around eyes; silver or blue eye shadow on cheeks and nose.

Dryer duct for arms; attach ribbons or cords to upper ends and tie them together across chest.

To make chest and back shields, cut two slightly-rounded triangular sheets from gray or blue poster board; punch holes at shoulders and crotch, tie the shields together using ribbons through holes. Curve neckhole for comfort. Draw designs with black marker or crayon.

Flatten two small, disposable, aluminium pie plates, punch holes in sides and use elastic bands through holes to tie around knees.

24. GHOST

White, loose-fitting, hooded robe from pattern L.

Paint face white, draw large black circles around eyes; green eyeshadow on lips and under eyes.

White gloves from pattern X-2.

25. GIFTBOX AND OTHER BOX COSTUMES

You need a square, lightweight box, to fit over child's body. Remove top for feet and turn the box upside down. Glue pretty paper or comic pages on each side and top. Cut holes for head and arms. Wrap wide ribbon (crepe paper or leftover fabric cut with pinking shears) around the box, gluing and tacking it securely in place. Tie a huge bow on child's head.

House: Remove top for feet, turn the box upside down and cut holes for head and arms. Make roof from poster board and attach it securely in place. Paint or glue details on house and roof.

Invent more box costumes. You can easily make a dice, puzzle cube, mailbox or television set.

Another great idea is a hot air balloon. Although it might be too cumbersome for trick-or-treating, it would make an eye-catching costume for a parade. Blow up a huge balloon (beach ball is great). Remove top and bottom from a suitable box. Attach the balloon above the box with long stiff wires taped around the balloon and twisted securely through holes in the box. The box covers child's body from knees to waist. Suspenders over shoulders attached to box hold it securely in place. Paint or glue designs on box for decorations.

26. GINGERBREAD MAN

Brown balaclava helmet from pattern W-2. Sew a large "candy" from two round pieces of white fabric; stuff with polyester filling, decorate with red ribbons, and attach it to the top of the balaclava helmet with an elastic chinstrap.

Brown tunic from pattern B and brown pants from pattern G, brown mittens from pattern X-1; sew or glue extra-wide white rickrack on costume. (You can make your own rickrack from any non-fraying fabric, such as felt.) Sew three large candy buttons (as for head candy), and attach them to front.

27. GNOME

Gnomes are folkloric dwarfs who live underground, guarding the treasures of earth.

Red cone-shaped fabric hat from pattern W-3, with white pom-pon (page 48) or little bell attached to top, elastic chinstrap. Gray yarn beard (page 46).

Green tunic from pattern B; tie rope around waist; attach little bells to rope ends. Red mittens from pattern X-1. Red pants from pattern G. Elasticized sleeve and leg ends. Red tote trimmed with white pom-pons and little bells.

28. HALLOWEENER

Make a helmet from large, round plastic container, cover´ it with orange self-adhesive vinyl. [Or make the helmet from orange poster board: Glue ends of rectangular piece together into a circle around head; cut face opening. Cut top circle, clipping around outside edge, and glue clipped edge under lower section.] Antennas from long, black pipe cleaners. Add elastic chinstrap.

Poncho: Cut a large circle from orange vinyl or fabric to reach from wrist to wrist between child's outstretched arms; cut a hole in the middle for head and cut a fringe all around lower edge. Zigzagged strips of black construction paper are taped around helmet and onto poncho's shoulders.

Make a drawstring bag from orange fabric circle, padded with batting, glue or sew on facial features made from black felt.

29. HAWAIIAN HULA DANCER

Skintone bodysuit (pattern U) and tights. Yellow, purple and blue crepe paper flowers for lei and hair (see page 37). Hula skirt from green crepe paper (see page 38). Optional long black wig (see page 35]. Make a matching tote by decorating any bag with green shredded crepe paper and lei flowers.

30. INDIANS

Tribesman: Green and orange felt headdress with white crepe paper feathers (page 39). Brown blouse from pattern B; brown pants from pattern G. Cut long, wide strips of brown felt with fringe cut in outer edges and sew to sleeves, blouse front and pants' sides as shown; cover inner edges with green and orange rickrack or felt strips. Face is painted blue and red.

Maiden: Black braided wig (page 35). Make a hairband from brown felt with Velcro closure at back; glue or sew red and green felt triangles on the band for decoration; attach a solitary feather to the band. Lengthen pattern B to make brown robe, fringe hem and sleeve ends and trim them with red and green rickrack or felt strips. Wooden and glass beads tied to leather thonging or raffene (synthetic raffia) jewelry.

Shortcut for littlest Indian: Dress the child in an old sweatsuit or jeans and top. Cut two 10cm/4" wide brown felt strips long enough to run from neck to wrist; cut fringe in outer edge of each strip and tack them temporarily to sleeves as shown; tack colorful rickrack over inner edges. Cardboard spats from pattern Y-4, decorated with black markers, tied at back. Attach a few feathers to an elastic headband.

31. JAILBIRD

Facial scars done with lipstick and brow pencil, stubble with spiral mascara brush, or burned toothpick or cork. Black and white striped cap (pattern W-6). Black and white striped stretchy sweatsuit (pattern C) doubles as pyjamas. Draw numbers on white cardboard strips with black marker, and tack them to cap and blouse front. (If you want to make the costume from non-stretchy fabric, use pattern B for blouse, and pattern G for pants.)

32. JESTER

Medieval rulers kept jesters, dressed in particolored (i.e. having different colors in different parts), cheerful costumes, in their court for amusement and entertainment. Neck ruffle (pattern W-9), hat (pattern W-7). Decorate a regular sweatshirt by sticking colorful self-adhesive vinyl diamonds (or tack felt diamonds) on bodice and sleeves. Tights or tight pants. Striped bloomers (pattern M-1). Spats (pattern Y-2). Attach bells to hat points, neck ruffle points and toes.

Jester carries a fool's sceptre in his hand. Head: Stuff toes of an old white sock with crumbled facial tissue; tie string tightly around neck, attaching it at the same time to wand; draw facial features with black marker. Colorful, three-pointed hat (pattern W-8), bells on each tip. Gather upper edge of a piece of fabric with string and tie it at back for neck ruffle.

33. KNIGHT

Helmet from poster board (pattern W-10) covered with aluminium paper, decorated with permanent black marker; attach feather to top and add elastic chinstrap. Mustache (see page 46). Gray or brown tunic (pattern B). Gray cardboard crest (pattern Z-2), decorated with black marker and tacked to tunic front.

Cardboard sword (pattern Z-3) is covered with aluminium paper, felt scabbard (pattern Z-4) attached to belt (felt belt and aluminium-covered plastic buckle from pattern Z-5). Cardboard spats (pattern Y-4), covered with aluminium paper and decorated with permanent black marker are tied at back.

34. LITTLE RED RIDINGHOOD

Red hooded cape from pattern O. (Optional: Trim edges with white synthetic fur.) White turtleneck from pattern I, red miniskirt from pattern H-1.

Paint lips and cheeks red. Use a small basket for treats, or make one from small cardboard box, covering it with yellow construction paper and drawing lines with brown marker; fold a strip of construction paper several times to make a sturdy handle, and staple it securely in place.

35. MAGICIAN

Simsalabim...Abracadabra...

Top hat from black poster board (pattern W-11). Tie a red ribbon around hat. Cut black mustache from felt and stick it under nose with rolled-up plastic bandage. Black cape, red lining, with neck ruffle and drawstring from pattern K. White gloves (pattern X-2).

Wide red sash tied around waist. Black tote appliquéd or fabric painted. Carry a black stick for a wand, or make you own: Roll up a sheet of newspaper very tightly, then glue it closed; paint the wand black or wrap it with black self-adhesive vinyl or tape.

36. MAHARAJAH

Turban: Wrap a large scarf or towel around head, attach it securely with safety pins or temporary tacks. Attach a large, glittering brooch, or a pretty flashy button to front of turban as jewelry.

Black eyebrows painted with brow pencil. Mustache affixed to skin with rolled-up self-adhesive, stretchy bandage (see page 46).

Bright blue or red velvet, velour or brocade robe from pattern E; sideslits for comfort; decorate the front, hemline and sleeve ends with glittering metallic ribbons.

37. MEXICAN

A broad-brimmed hat with chinstrap. If you don't have a suitable hat, make one from cardboard and a paperbag (see cowboy). Mustache, see page 46.

Poncho: Cut a large rectangle from an old duffel blanket, felt or any suitable fabric. Cut a lengthwise slit of about 56cm/22" long in the center for head. Trim all edges with bias tape or foldover braid. Glue or sew colorful strips of felt or ribbons to lower edges for decoration; attach fringe made from craft yarn (see page 47).

For a serenade, make guitar from cardboard box, paper towel tube, and some string; collect treats in its hole.

38. MUMMY

Paint face white. White mittens from pattern X-1. White pants or shorts.

Cut any white fabric (old sheet, drapes etc.) into long strips of about 10 cm (4") wide each. Wrap child's arms, then body, overlapping strips a bit, attaching each strip-end securely to the next one by tying ends together, or using safety pins or by sewing. Wrap legs and head.

(Arrange wrapping so that the child is able to go to the bathroom in this costume.)

39. OCTOPUS

Balloon-based papier-mâché helmet (page 41), painted pink or brown. Add elastic chinstrap to hold it securely in place.

Sew eight pink or brown arms from pattern N (or use different color underneath); stuff each lightly with polyester filling. Sew a neckband from ribknit and attach arms to it, overlapping each one, so they fit around the band evenly. Three arms will be at front, three at back, and one over each arm of child; attach these two to child's wrists with straps sewn underneath. Tack felt circles to tentacles for suckers.

Sew or glue octopus design on a tote bag.

40.PEPPERMINT CANDY

Use red and white candy-striped and solid green or red colors to make the costume and hat.

Top hat is made from cardboard with pattern W-11, and covered with fabric. Tunic from pattern A, with self-ruffled sleeve ends and a bow tied on front. Shorten pattern G to make knee-length pants. Lace trim.

Sew a matching tote from leftover fabrics.

41. PETER PAN

Green felt hat from pattern W-12; attach a feather to back.

Green tunic from pattern P has elasticized waist.

Green pantyhose, or sweatpants (pattern C-2); or wear jeans. Green felt spats with curvy toes from pattern Y-2, tied around ankles.

Green totebag; affix "magic pixie dust" all over the bag by gluing some glitter and a star on it.

42. PIERROT

This sad clown will melt your heart. All black-and-white.

Black or white cap from pattern W-6. Paint face white; sad eyebrows and one solitary black-framed teardrop drawn with brow pencil, tiny mouth.

White ruffle with lower edge trimmed with black bias tape, elasticized neck (pattern F-2).

Tunic from pattern A, pants from pattern M-1; cut right sleeve, right side of top and left leg from black fabric, and the rest from white fabric.

White gloves from pattern X-2.

43. PIRATE

Red-and-white polkadot scarf tied around head. Cut an earring from paper towel tube, wrap it with aluminium foil, and hang around ear with cord. Eyepatch: Glue elastic strap between two felt circles. Mustache (page 46). Facial scars done with makeup crayon.

Big white shirt (pattern A). Black belt. Black or yellow vest (pattern J). Tack white felt skull and crossbones on the vest. Cardboard sword in felt scabbard (patterns Z-3, Z-4). Cardboard spats (pattern Y-4). "Gold" chains and other flashy costume jewelry around neck. (Black cardboard treasure coffin; decorate it with white skull and crossbones, attach a sturdy handle and cut a large hole in top for treats.)

44. PRINCE

Cover round plastic container with gold metallic paper, cut it into a crown, attach elastic chinstrap; glue on a few glittery red and blue buttons for crown jewels.

White shirt from shiny fabric (pattern A). Blue vest from metallic fabric or brocade (pattern J). Cut two long strips from vest fabric and tack them temporarily to jeans' sideseams. Red cape from pattern K, trimmed with gold metallic ribbons or white fake fur. Cut a long scarf from red fabric and tie it around waist as a sash.

45. PRINCESS

Glue yellow metallic paper on cardboard and cut crown from it with pattern W-15. Attach elastic chinstrap to hold the crown securely in place. Glue glitter all around the crown.

Gown from pattern A. Cut decorative slits up from sleeve ends and sew stretched elastic at midarms. Trim the gown with lace, metallic braid, ribbons and sequins. Tie metallic braid around waist.

46. PUMPKIN

Orange cap from pattern W-6; roll a piece of black felt tightly for a stem, tack it closed and attach on top of cap; for hair, sew strands of orange or black craft yarn around cap's lower edge. (Black pants and top.)

Orange barrel costume from pattern Q-1 with armholes, elasticized neck and lower edge. Metal wire or polyester boning tacked inside, around costume waist, holds it out from body. Appliqué or glue on jack-o'-lantern's facial features made from black felt.

From leftover fabric, sew a matching orange tote for treats and glue facial features on it, made from black felt.

47. ROBIN HOOD

Robin Hood is a story-book outlaw who robbed the rich and gave to the poor.

Green felt hat with elastic chinstrap from pattern W-13; attach a long feather to one side. Green shoulder cloak made from felt or crepe paper (pattern R-1). Green tunic from pattern B, brown belt.

Brown shoulder bag for treats (pattern R-2); brown tights; brown spats (pattern Y-2) tied around ankles.

48. ROBOT

You need one box to fit over the body and a smaller box to fit over the head. Cut face and neck holes in smaller box; remove top from bigger box for feet, turn the box upside down and cut holes for arms and head.

Cover both boxes with aluminium paper. Glue boxes together. Wind metal wire or floral wire around pen for antennas; twist ends through holes in the box. Glue on corks and bottle caps for knobs. Glue a black keyhole and a cardboard key on shoulder.

Dryer ducts for arms; tie them together with cord across chest.

49. SANTA CLAUS

Red cap (pattern W-3); white pom-pon (page 48) at top; white fake fur trim around lower edge. White eyebrows and beard from fake fur (see page 46). Red tunic (pattern B); white pom-pons for "buttons" and fake fur trim around sleeve ends. Black belt around waist. White mittens (pattern X-1). Red pants (pattern G). Black knee-high spats from poster board tied behind legs (pattern Y-4). Red drawstring bag for treats.

50. SCARECROW

Old clothes (or tunic from pattern B, pants from pattern G; add patches and buttons). Tie bunches of raffene or jute strands to elastic hairband; add an old hat on top. Black circles around eyes and mouth. Scarf around neck.

Make four fringed bands; one for each wrist and ankle. For each band, wind brown raffene around stiff cardboard (20cm x 20cm, or 8" x 8"), strands tightly side-by-side; stick masking tape on both sides, bend cardboard and pull it out; cut a 38cm/15" long piece of twill tape and machine stitch it across the center to hold all raffene strands together, leaving ends for ties; pull masking tape off. Fold all raffene loops to one side, cut loops open, and tie the fringed bands around wrists and ankles under sleeve and leg ends.

51. SKELETON

White balaclava helmet from pattern W-2. White face, black around eyes, on nose and lips.

Black tunic from pattern B and black pants from pattern G. Cut simple bones, as shown, from white self-adhesive vinyl and press them directly onto costume (they can be removed later to use the outfit as pyjamas or other costumes). Instead of self-adhesive vinyl, cut the bones from white felt and tack them temporarily in place. (Optional: Black gloves from pattern X-2; glue white fingerbones on gloves.) Black treat bag with white skull and crossbones from vinyl or felt for decoration.

52. SNIPS

These creatures from a faraway planet are entirely blue and silver.

Hat from disposable aluminium pie plate: Cut a slit from edge to center, staple cut edges together, overlapping slightly to form a pointy hat; twist two long strips of aluminium foil into antennas; add elastic chinstrap; glue or staple strips of zigzagged metallic paper around hat's lower edge for hair. Face painted with blue strokes. Blue circular cape (see Halloweener) made of vinyl, lower edge cut in points. Glue aluminium foil decals and glitter on cape and tote bag.

53. SNOWMAN

Top hat from black poster board (pattern W-11).

Face painted 'white, black around eyes and lips. Carrot nose from orange construction paper (pattern W-17), stick it on clean, dry nose with rolled-up plastic bandage.

White barrel costume from pattern Q-2, has elasticized neck, waist and hem. Black felt circles glued on front for buttons. White mittens from pattern X-1. Long, colorful scarf tied around neck.

Decorate a tote bag with a snowman motif cut from white and black felt scraps.

54. STAR

Star is made from two sheets of yellow poster board, or yellow metallic paper glued on poster board (pattern W-14); points glued together except for lower edge which is left open for neck. Glue glitter and sequins on each point, attach some rays made from tinsel or zigzagged metallic paper.

Blue or yellow gown from pattern A; decorate with glitter, sequins, and metallic ribbons. Sideslits for comfort.

55. TOY SOLDIER

Red hat with black brim made from poster board (pattern W-4), braided cord chinstrap.

Red tunic from pattern B; black belt and ribbons across chest. The easiest way to make the belt and ribbons is to cut them from black self-adhesive vinyl and stick them directly on costume. Yellow ribbon trim on sleeve ends. White pants from pattern G, with black ribbon trim (self-adhesive vinyl) along side seams. Knee-high spats from black poster board tied at back (pattern Y-4).

56. TREE

Brown balaclava helmet from pattern W-2; tack green felt leaves all over, overlapping each leaf a bit, to cover the helmet.

Brown circular cape (see Halloweener) covered with green felt leaves. Cut the leaves from felt, or other non-fraying fabric, or vinyl, and sew or glue them in place at stem end only.

Use different shades of green for an interesting effect, or make it an autumn tree by using yellow, orange and red leaves shaped like maple or oak leaves etc.

57. TROLL

Ragged jute wig (page 34); unravel jute and backcomb it for a messy effect; spray heavily with hairspray. Nose is a section from an egg container, paint it red and stick it on nose with rolled-up plastic bandage. "Dirt" on face with brown and black makeup. Burlap top (pattern B) and pants (pattern G); leave all cut edges unfinished to unravel a bit; add colorful patches. A braided tail from jute tied around waist under the top.

58. VIKING

Vikings, legendary Norsemen, were daring Scandinavian pirates who roamed the seas. They were the best seamen and shipbuilders of their time and terrorized nearly all of Europe.

Helmet (pattern W-18) is made from gray cardboard, with white horns. Yellow craft yarn glued around helmet's lower edge for hair. Yellow mustache and beard (see page 46). Brown tunic (pattern B), brown pants (pattern G). Sword (pattern Z-3), scabbard (pattern Z-4), belt (pattern Z-5), shield (pattern W-16), and spats (pattern Y-4), are all made from gray posterboard and decorated with black marker. Tack the round shield on front of treat bag.

59. WITCH

Hat made from black poster board (pattern W-3). Attach black yarn hair around crown's lower edge, unravel it, tease and spray with hairspray (or tie yarn strands around elastic hairband). Black makeup around eyes and lips. Long nose (pattern W-17) from skintone construction paper (cut adequate space for nostrils) attached on nose with rolledup plastic bandage.

Black drawstring cape from pattern K; sew or glue on a yellow moon and a black cat for decoration. Gown from pattern A. Cut long nails from wax or plastic container, apply them over nails with masking tape; paint with dark red nail varnish, or cover with self-adhesive, red vinyl. Make a treat pot with a handle by cutting a large plastic container; glue black construction paper or self-adhesive vinyl around the pot and handle.

60. XMAS TREE

Green costume from pattern S; branches sewn together, openings at sides for arms, bottom left open for feet. Polyester boning tacked inside, around hemline, holds lower edge stiff.

Decorate the tree with damaged and discarded Christmas tree decorations and garlands, or make a few from felt, self-adhesive vinyl, metallic paper and crepe paper. Attach decorations securely so they won't fly away in wind.

LAST-MINUTE COSTUMES

It happens to all of us once in a while;
we are too busy to even think about
costumes and suddenly it's Halloween.
If you have collected a few costumes
and props in a dress-up trunk along
the year, it's a snap to throw something
together in minutes. Consider these
fourteen panic solutions and let your
children invent more.

ACCIDENT-PRONE KID

Paint sad scars on face with lipstick
and brow pencil. Cut sole off of one
old, white sportsock, leaving a strap
underfoot and pull it on the "broken
leg" to cover the shoe under "cast";
wrap that leg with any white cloth or
towel, tie securely or use safety pins.
Also wrap head with white cloth, scarf
or towel. Fold a large white scarf or
a small tablecloth into triangular
bandage, and tie it behind the neck
to carry the "broken arm".

BABY

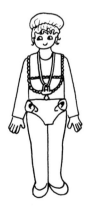

Dress the child in skintone bodysuit
and tights, or sweatsuit. If you have
a new baby in the family, you will have
bonnet, bib and other props for this
costume. Or make a quick bonnet: Cut
a circle from fabric (diameter 51 cm
or 20"); trim edge with lace (sew or
glue); stitch stretched elastic around
head 7.5 cm (3") from the edge, forming
self-ruffle. (No time to sew? Use a
shower cap, or knot four corners of
handkerchief for a cute cap.) Quick
bib: Use kitchen towel; fold lower edge
upward for a pocket, attach sides with
safety pins; roll upper end tightly
around long ribbon or cord several times
and then tie ribbon ends behind neck.
Tie pacifier or rattle to ribbon around
neck. Fold white towel or scarf into
a diaper, and attach sides with large
safety pins or knots.

BALLOON TREE

Dress the child in sweatsuit, or jeans and jacket. Add elastic hairband. Blow up lots of balloons and attach them around the child, at hairband, top and sleeves, with small safety pins. Arrange balloons so that they don't affect visibility.

DOCTOR

Headlight: Cut a circle out of an aluminium pie plate, paint on yellow rays with poster paints or acrylic paints; or glue a sparkling button in the middle for "light"; attach it to elastic headband. Use a toy stethoscope or make your own: Tie cord around neck with ends knotted inside a funnel (or plastic bottle top, cut like a funnel). White coat is father's shirt; shorten sleeves temporarily by basting pleats at midarms. Add a thermometer and tongue depressor, made of cardboard, and leave it showing from the pocket.

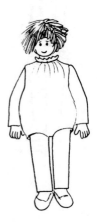

GARBAGE BAG

Cut legholes in the bottom of a garbage bag; pull the bag on and cut armholes. Fill the bag with lightweight polyester stuffing or crumpled papers. Gather upper edge around neck with masking tape. Facial makeup: Stubble done with spiral mascara brush, or burned toothpick or cork; "dirt" on cheeks and forehead using gray makeup. Backcomb hair and spray it with hairspray.

LADY

Fancy old hat with flowers and feathers. Mother's old dress tied at waist with belt or elastic ribbon; sleeves and hem temporarily shortened (fabric tape or basting is fast). Lots of costume jewelry. Grownup facial makeup; paint nails or use lacy gloves, if you have them. Huge scarf with fringes tied around shoulders as a shawl. Pretty purse.

MONSTERS

Paper bag monster: A large brown grocery bag fits nicely over a small child for a one-piece costume. Cut holes for face and arms, glue or paint on designs; glue on papercup ears and yarn hair. Facial makeup. Two-piece costume for an older child: Cut armholes and neckhole in grocery bag, and use a smaller paper bag for the head, cutting it into a helmet to leave face free; tape the bag securely in place with masking tape, or add chinstrap. Draw designs with markers, glue on ears and shredded hair made from construction paper. Draw black circles around mouth and eyes.

Plastic bag monster: Pull one large upside-down garbage bag over shoulders (after you have cut opening for head and slits for hands). Shred lower edge. Pull another large bag over head and shoulders (after you have cut opening for face); gather up the bag with masking tape around neck and above head; shred bottom and top as shown. Spooky face with black and green makeup crayons; black mustache, or row of pointy teeth, and brows, all made from construction paper, and attached with rolled-up plastic bandages.

NURSE

To create an old-fashioned nurse headdress, cut a large semicircle from white fabric or crepe paper (diameter 76cm/30") to go around head and tie at the back. White dress is father's shirt; sleeves temporarily shortened by basting pleats at midarms, tucks at shoulders; belt tied around waist. White plastic bag for treats. Cut three red crosses from fabric or cardboard and glue or baste them on front of pocket, headdress and bag.

OLD WOMAN

Adult-sized jacket or coat (sleeves shortened temporarily). A large, fringed scarf tied around shoulders. Little old purse. A smaller scarf on head, tied under chin babushka-style. Spectacles on nose: Remove lenses from old sunglasses, or make the frames from black pipe cleaners or floral wire.

PAPERBOY

Glue pages from your local newspaper around brown grocery bag. Cut neckhole and armholes. To make a hat, fold a sheet of newspaper in half; fold upper corners to meet in the middle; fold front and back lower edges to outside, leaving an opening for head. Add elastic chinstrap, attaching ends securely to both sides.

 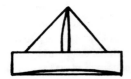

STRANGERS FROM MARS

Boy: Cover colander with crinkled foil, attach elastic chinstrap, add antennas made from twisted aluminium paper. Take four small disposable aluminium plates, punch two holes in each and attach with elastic ties around shoulders and knees. Decorate a large, disposable aluminium roasting pan with corks and bottlecaps and strips of black tape; punch holes for elastic ties and attach pan on chest around neck and waist. Facial makeup.

Girl: The costume and helmet are made from bright yellow or red, paper-backed aluminium foil. For a small size, you need a sheet of 100x66cm (39x26"), for medium/large size, you need a sheet of 150x66cm (60x26"). Cut the sheet in half lengthwise, one half for the costume, the other for helmet. Costume: Fold the sheet in half at shoulders, cut neckhole with front slit; shred lower edges and curl each strand by pulling it against a blade; tie belt or strong ribbon around waist. Helmet: Cut a piece 56x33cm (22x13"); staple it into a circle to fit snugly around head; cut opening for face in front; shred both lower and upper edges and curl them like hem. Decorate costume and helmet with permanent, black marker. Facial makeup. (If you don't have paper-backed aluminium foil, try making this costume from heavy-duty crepe paper, with helmet section glued over poster board; or from household aluminium foil glued over brown paper. Crepe paper and aluminium foil can be curled up by rolling strands around a pencil.)

VAGABOND

This Halloween Hobo wears old, ragged clothes and a hat; add a few quick, colorful patches by basting or attaching them with fabric tape. Stubble created with spiral mascara brush, or rubbing with burned toothpick or cork. Treat bag from a bright scarf; tie each two opposite corners together around lightweight plastic bowl, leaving easy opening at top for treats.

PATTERNS

PATTERN A: GOWN OR TUNIC (Angel, Bride, Fairy, Flower, Friar, Peppermint Candy, Pierrot, Pirate, Prince, Princess, Star, Witch)

Very loose-fitting gown, or tunic, with raglan sleeves and elasticized neck. Light or mediumweight cotton-type fabrics. Fabric required for gown: 125(190)210cm x 115(140)140cm, or 50(75)82" x 45(55)55"; for tunic: 115(140)150cm x 115(140)140cm, or 45(55)60" x 45(55)55". Elastic, bias tape.

Sewing: Stitch raglan sleeves to bodice front and back. Stitch sides and underarms. Sew bias tape casing around neck, leaving an opening; insert narrow elastic through casing. Press sleeve ends and hem allowance under and topstitch in place. Tunic: Bias tape casing and elastic around sleeve ends. Pierrot: Cut sleeves 10cm/4" longer, stitch stretched elastic around wrists to form self-ruffled sleeve ends.

PATTERN B: TUNIC (Drummer, Gingerbread Man, Gnome, Indians, Knight, Robin Hood, Santa Claus, Scarecrow, Skeleton, Toy Soldier, Troll, Viking)

Loose-fitting straight top with long sleeves. Mediumweight cotton-type fabrics. Fabric required: 90(115)125cm x 115cm, or 35(45)50" x 45". Extra fabric required for knight costume's hand guards: 40(45)45cm x 115cm, or 16(18)18" x 45".

Sewing: Stitch shoulder seams of tunic and neck facing; stitch facing around neck, press under and stitch in place. (Instead of facing, you may trim neck with bias tape.) Stitch sleeves to bodice, and then stitch sides and underarms. Overlock sleeve ends and hem edge, press them under and stitch in place. Indian maiden: Lengthen the pattern to make a dress. Knight: Shorten sleeves 5cm/2"; stitch hand guard ends together into a circle (stitching each of the four separately); stitch each pair together along lower edge, turn right side out and press; turn sleeves inside out and stitch hand guards around sleeve ends.

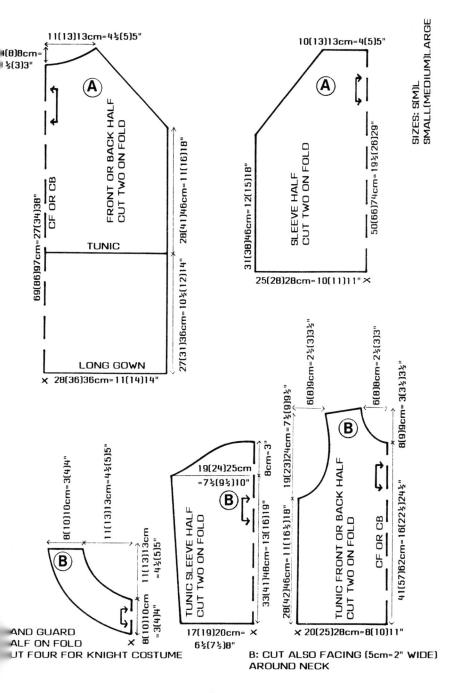

11[13]13cm=4½[5]5"

[8]8cm= ½[3]3"

(A)

FRONT OR BACK HALF
CUT TWO ON FOLD

CF OR CB

69[86]97cm=27[34]38"

TUNIC

27[31]36cm=10½[12]14"

28[41]46cm=11[16]18"

LONG GOWN

× 28[36]36cm=11[14]14"

10[13]13cm=4[5]5"

(A)

SLEEVE HALF
CUT TWO ON FOLD

31[38]46cm=12[15]18"

50[66]74cm=19½[26]29"

25[28]28cm=10[11]11" ×

SIZES: S[M]L
SMALL[MEDIUM]LARGE

8[10]10cm=3[4]4"

11[13]13cm=4½[5]5"

(B)

11[13]13cm =4½[5]5"

8[10]10cm =3[4]4"

19[24]25cm =7½[9½]10"

(B)

8cm=3"

TUNIC SLEEVE HALF
CUT TWO ON FOLD

33[41]48cm=13[16]19"

17[19]20cm= 6½[7½]8" ×

6[8]9cm=2½[3]3½"

6[8]8cm=2½[3]3"

(B)

19[23]24cm=7½[9]9½"

8[9]9cm=3[3½]3½"

TUNIC FRONT OR BACK HALF
CUT TWO ON FOLD

CF OR CB

28[42]46cm=11[16½]18"

41[57]62cm=16[22½]24½"

× 20[25]28cm=8[10]11"

AND GUARD
ALF ON FOLD
UT FOUR FOR KNIGHT COSTUME

B: CUT ALSO FACING [5cm=2" WIDE]
AROUND NECK

91

PATTERNS C: SWEATSUIT (Bat, Jailbird)

Loose-fitting sweatshirt with long raglan sleeves, ribknit trim. Easy pull-on pants without side seams, elasticized waist, ribknit ankles. Stretchy fabrics only, such as stretch terry or velour, cotton knit, sweatsuit fabrics. Fabric required for sweatsuit: 100(150)210cm x 150cm, or 40(60)82" x 60", plus ribknit: 25(40)40cm x 90cm, or 10(15)15" x 36".

C-1 Sweatshirt: Stitch raglan sleeves to bodice front and back. Stitch sides and underarms. Turn the garment and sleeves inside out. Stitch ribknit bands into circles, fold in half lengthwise right sides out, and stitch them around sleeve ends, neck and waist, stretching the bands to divide fabric fullness evenly.

C-2 Pull-on pants: Stitch center front and center back seams. Stitch inner leg seams. Sew a casing around waist, leaving an opening; insert elastic through opening and stitch ends together; distribute fullness evenly, and stitch elastic to center front and back seams, through casing, to prevent it from rolling. Stitch ribknit bands into circles, fold in half lengthwise right sides out and stitch them around legs, stretching the bands to divide fabric fullness evenly.

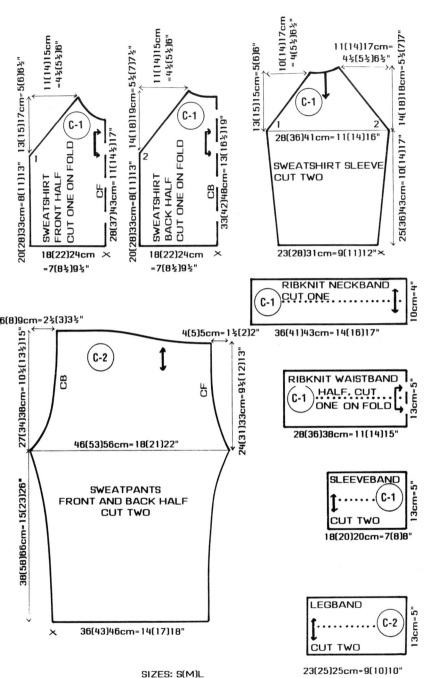

SWEATSHIRT FRONT HALF CUT ONE ON FOLD

11(14)15cm = 4½(5½)6"

13(15)17cm=5(6)6½"

20(28)33cm=8(11)13"

28(37)43cm=11(14½)17"

CF

18(22)24cm × =7(8½)9½"

SWEATSHIRT BACK HALF CUT ONE ON FOLD

11(14)15cm =4½(5½)6"

14(18)19cm=5½(7)7½"

20(28)33cm=8(11)13"

33(42)48cm=13(16½)19"

CB

18(22)24cm × =7(8½)9½"

SWEATSHIRT SLEEVE CUT TWO

10(14)17cm = 4½(5½)6½"

11(14)17cm= 4½(5½)6½"

13(15)15cm=5(6)6"

14(18)18cm=5½(7)7"

25(36)43cm=10(14)17"

28(36)41cm=11(14)16"

23(28)31cm=9(11)12"×

RIBKNIT NECKBAND CUT ONE

C-1

10cm=4"

36(41)43cm=14(16)17"

RIBKNIT WAISTBAND HALF CUT ONE ON FOLD

C-1

13cm=5"

28(36)38cm=11(14)15"

SLEEVEBAND CUT TWO

C-1

13cm=5"

18(20)20cm=7(8)8"

LEGBAND CUT TWO

C-2

13cm=5"

23(25)25cm=9(10)10"

6(8)9cm=2½(3)3½"

4(5)5cm=1½(2)2"

27(34)38cm=10½(13½)15"

24(31)33cm=9½(12)13"

CB

CF

46(53)56cm=18(21)22"

38(58)66cm=15(23)26"

SWEATPANTS FRONT AND BACK HALF CUT TWO

× 36(43)46cm=14(17)18"

SIZES: S(M)L
SMALL(MEDIUM)LARGE

93

PATTERN D: COVERALLS (Astronaut, Bunny, Cat, Chef, Clown, Mouse)

Loose-fitting coveralls, long raglan sleeves, ribknit band or drawstring neck, ribknit or elastic around sleeve ends and legs, zipper on front. For animal costumes, use fake fur (old car seat covers), velour, soft and fleecy fabrics; for astronaut nylon or quilted fabrics; for chef lightweight, white fabrics (old sheet); for clown any bright colored, lightweight fabrics. Fabric required: 165(215)240cm x 115(140)140cm, or 65(85)95" x 45(55)55"; plus ribknit 50x56cm or 20x22". (Buy extra fabric for accessories.) Zipper, elastic, bias tape, polyester stuffing.

Sewing: Stitch center front seam below zipper; sew zipper in place. Stitch center back seam, inner leg seams, underarms, and then raglan sleeves to armholes. Stitch ribknit bands around neck, sleeve ends and legs (see sweatshirt), or use elastic instead of ribknit. Clown: Cut leg and sleeve ends 10cm/4" longer; sew bias tape casing around neck and insert drawstring through casing; hem sleeve and leg ends narrowly, stitch stretched elastic to them, 8cm/3" from lower edges, forming self-ruffles. Animal tails: Sew tail, leaving upper end open, turn right side out, fill with polyester stuffing (or fabric scraps); stitch the tail into center back seam below waist. (Fake fur tail: Roll a tail-length of fabric until desired thickness; tack through and through.)

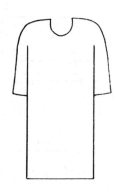

PATTERN E: ROBE (Bedouin, Maharajah)

Long, loose-fitting robe with kimono sleeves. Front slits for bedouin, and long side slits for maharajah. Lightweight fabrics (old curtains, bedspreads, sheets). Fabric required: 150(210)230cm x 115(140)150cm, or 60(82)90" x 45(55)60". Bias tape.

Sewing: Stitch shoulder seams, sides and underarms. Stitch doublefold bias tape around neck. Press sleeve ends, hem allowance and side slits under and stitch in place. Bedouin: Trim slits with bias tape.

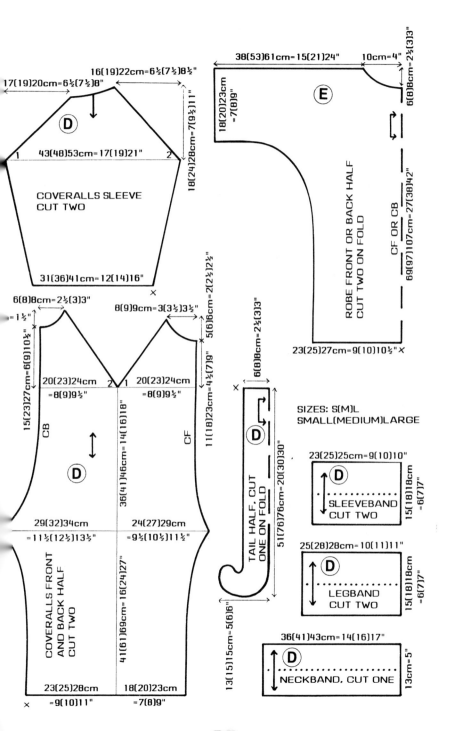

17(19)20cm=6½(7½)8"

16(19)22cm=6½(7½)8½"

D

1   43(48)53cm=17(19)21"   2

18(24)28cm=7(9½)11"

COVERALLS SLEEVE
CUT TWO

31(36)41cm=12(14)16"

38(53)61cm=15(21)24"   10cm=4"

E

18(20)23cm=7(8)9"

6(8)8cm=2½(3)3"

ROBE FRONT OR BACK HALF
CUT TWO ON FOLD

CF OR CB

69(97)107cm=27(38)42"

23(25)27cm=9(10)10½"×

6(8)8cm=2½(3)3"

8(9)9cm=3(3½)3½"

5(6)6cm=2(2½)2½"

=1½"

15(23)27cm=6(9)10½"

20(23)24cm
=8(9)9½"

2 1

20(23)24cm
=8(9)9½"

11(18)23cm=4½(7)9"

CB

CF

D

36(41)46cm=14(16)18"

TAIL HALF, CUT
ONE ON FOLD

51(76)76cm=20(30)30"

6(8)8cm=2½(3)3"

D

SIZES: S(M)L
SMALL(MEDIUM)LARGE

23(25)25cm=9(10)10"

D

SLEEVEBAND
CUT TWO

15(18)18cm
=6(7)7"

29(32)34cm
=11½(12½)13½"

24(27)29cm
=9½(10½)11½"

D

COVERALLS FRONT
AND BACK HALF
CUT TWO

41(61)69cm=16(24)27"

25(28)28cm=10(11)11"

D

LEGBAND
CUT TWO

15(18)18cm
=6(7)7"

23(25)28cm
=9(10)11"

18(20)23cm
=7(8)9"

13(15)15cm=5(6)6"

36(41)43cm=14(16)17"

D

NECKBAND, CUT ONE

13cm=5"

95

PATTERNS F: BUMBLEBEE COSTUME AND NECK RUFFLE (Neck ruffle also for Pierrot)

Ruffle has elasticized neck opening, costume has zipper on front. For bumblebee, use soft fabrics with nap, such as fake fur, velour, terry, fleece, velveteen; any lightweight, white fabric for Pierrot. Costume: 60(85)90cm x 90cm, or 23(32)36" x 36"; neck ruffle: 23(28)31cm x 115cm, or 9(11)12" x 45". Elastic, zipper, doublefold bias tape.

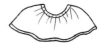

F-1 Costume: Sew doublefold bias tape around armholes, neck and hem edge. Stitch shoulder seams. Stitch separating zipper to front.
F-2 Neck ruffle: Stitch shoulder seams. Trim lower edge with bias tape. Sew wide bias tape casing around neck and insert elastic through casing.

PATTERN G: PULL-ON PANTS (Gingerbread Man, Gnome, Indian, Peppermint Candy, Santa Claus, Scarecrow, Skeleton, Troll, Viking, Toy Soldier)

Loose-fitting pull-on pants without side seams made from non-stretchy fabrics, elasticized waist. (Knee-length drawers for Peppermint Candy.) Fabric required: 75(100)115cm x 115(115)140cm, or 30(40)45" x 45(45)55". Elastic, lace.

Sewing: Stitch center front and back seams, then inner leg seams. Press leg ends under and stitch in place. Stitch casing around waist and insert elastic through casing. Gnome's pants have elasticized leg ends. Peppermint Candy: Trim leg ends with lace.

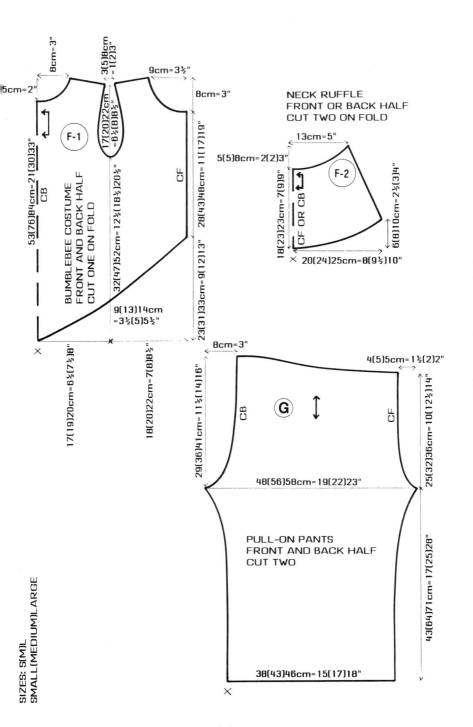

8cm=3"

3(5)8cm = 1(2)3"

9cm=3½"

5cm=2"

8cm=3"

F-1

17(20)22cm = 6½(8)8½"

NECK RUFFLE
FRONT OR BACK HALF
CUT TWO ON FOLD

53(76)84cm=21(30)33"
CB

13cm=5"

5(5)8cm=2(2)3"

F-2

18(23)23cm=7(9)9"
CF OR CB

6(8)10cm=2½(3)4"

BUMBLEBEE COSTUME
FRONT AND BACK HALF
CUT ONE ON FOLD

32(47)52cm=12½(18½)20½"

28(43)48cm=11(17)19"
CF

20(24)25cm=8(9½)10"

23(31)33cm=9(12)13"

9(13)14cm
=3½(5)5½"

8cm=3"

4(5)5cm=1½(2)2"

17(19)20cm=6½(7½)8"

18(20)22cm=7(8)8½"

29(36)41cm=11½(14)16"
CB

G

CF

25(32)36cm=10(12½)14"

48(56)58cm=19(22)23"

PULL-ON PANTS
FRONT AND BACK HALF
CUT TWO

43(64)71cm=17(25)28"

38(43)46cm=15(17)18"

SIZES: S(M)L
SMALL(MEDIUM)LARGE

97

PATTERNS H: MINISKIRT & PANTIES
(Cheerleader, Little Red Ridinghood)

Circular miniskirt has elasticized waistband. Panties in stretchy fabrics only; elasticized waist, ribknit legbands. Fabric required for miniskirt: 85(105)120cm x 90(115)115cm, or 32(40)46" x 36(45)45"; for panties: 51(62)64cm x 30(36)40cm, or 20(24)25" x 12(14)15"; plus ribknit 10x90cm, or 4x36". Wide elastic.

H-1 Miniskirt: Stitch waistband into a circle, leaving an opening in the seam for elastic; fold the band in half lengthwise right side out, and stitch it around skirt's upper edge. Insert elastic through waistband opening, and sew ends together. Press hem under and stitch in place.

H-2 Panties: Stitch side seams. Overlock upper edge, press it under about 2.5cm/1" and stitch down, to form a casing, leaving an opening. Insert elastic through casing and stitch ends together. Turn panties inside out. Stitch ribknit bands into circles, fold in half lengthwise right sides out, and stitch them around legholes.

PATTERN I: TURTLENECK (Cheerleader, Little Red Ridinghood)

Straight top with turtleneck collar, long sleeves gathered at caps. Stretchy fabrics only, such as cotton knit, stretch terry, velour. Fabric required: 65(100)115cm x 140cm, or 25(40)45" x 55".

Sewing: Stitch shoulder seams. Gather sleeve tops, and stitch them to bodice. Stitch sides and underarms. Press sleeve ends and hem under and topstitch in place. Turn the garment inside out. Stitch turtleneck collar into a circle, fold in half lengthwise right side out, and stitch it around neck. Cheerleader: Cut a huge monogram from felt or poster board, and baste it temporarily on front.

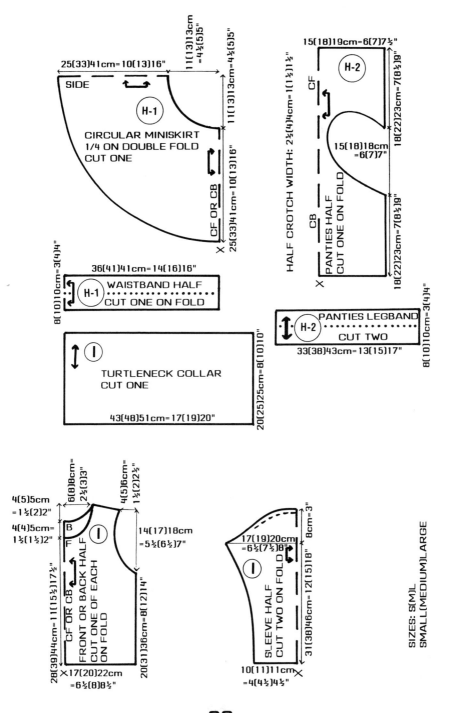

25(33)41cm=10(13)16"

11(13)13cm =4½(5)5"

SIDE

H-1

CIRCULAR MINISKIRT
1/4 ON DOUBLE FOLD
CUT ONE

11(13)13cm=4½(5)5"

CF OR CB

25(33)41cm=10(13)16"

X

8(10)10cm=3(4)4"

H-1

36(41)41cm=14(16)16"

WAISTBAND HALF
CUT ONE ON FOLD

I

TURTLENECK COLLAR
CUT ONE

20(25)25cm=8(10)10"

43(48)51cm=17(19)20"

HALF CROTCH WIDTH: 2½(4)4cm=1(1½)1½"

15(18)19cm=6(7)7½"

H-2

CF

18(22)23cm=7(8½)9"

15(18)18cm =6(7)7"

CB

18(22)23cm=7(8½)9"

PANTIES HALF
CUT ONE ON FOLD

X

H-2

PANTIES LEGBAND
CUT TWO

33(38)43cm=13(15)17"

8(10)10cm=3(4)4"

4(5)5cm =1½(2)2"

6(8)8cm= 2½(3)3"

4(5)6cm= 1½(2)2½"

4(4)5cm= 1½(1½)2"

B

F

I

14(17)18cm =5½(6½)7"

CF OR CB

FRONT OR BACK HALF
CUT ONE OF EACH
ON FOLD

28(39)44cm=11(15½)17½"

20(31)36cm=8(12)14"

X 17(20)22cm =6½(8)8½"

17(19)20cm =6½(7½)8"

8cm=3"

I

SLEEVE HALF
CUT TWO ON FOLD

31(38)46cm=12(15)18"

10(11)11cm X =4(4½)4½"

SIZES: S(M)L
SMALL(MEDIUM)LARGE

99

PATTERN J: VEST (Cowboy, Pirate, Prince)

Unlined or lined one-piece vest without side seams. Synthetic leather or suede, corduroy, quilted fabrics; (velveteen, brocade or metallic fabrics - with lining - for Prince). Fabric required: 40(55)60cm x 90cm, or 15(20)22" x 36"; plus the same quantity for lining. Bias tape.

Sewing: Unlined: Stitch doublefold bias tape all around raw edges of armholes, neck, front and lower edge. Stitch shoulder seams. Lined: Stitch vest and lining together around armholes and all edges, except shoulders, leaving an opening at hem center back. Trim and clip all corners and curves. Turn garment right side out and press. Slipstitch hem opening closed. Stitch shoulder seams.

PATTERN K: CAPE (Devil, Frankenstein, Magician, Prince, Witch)

Unlined or lined, semi-circular cape with or without neck ruffle, drawstring closure. (If your fabric is not wide enough, make seam at center back.) Lightweight fabrics, such as cotton and blends, nylon, velvet, velveteen. Fabric required: 160(210)225cm x 90(115)115cm, or 62(80)86" x 36(45)45". Cord.

Sewing: Unlined, with neck ruffle: Press front edges and hem allowance under and stitch in place. Press neck ruffle ends under, and stitch in place; fold ruffle in half right side out and stitch it to cape around neck. To form casing in neck ruffle for drawstring, stitch 1.3cm/½" above neck seam, through both thicknesses, leaving ends open; insert cord through casing to tie at front; sew cord in place to casing ends so it will not pull out. Lined: Sew lining to cape around front edges and hem, leaving neck open. Turn right side out and press. Stitch neck ruffle as above. Without neck ruffle: Sew wide bias tape casing around neck for cord.

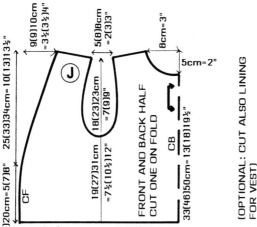

9(9)10cm =3½(3½)4"

5(8)8cm =2(3)3"

8cm=3"

5cm=2"

25(33)34cm= 10(13)13½"

J

18(23)23cm =7(9)9"

CF

19(27)31cm =7½(10½)12"

FRONT AND BACK HALF CUT ONE ON FOLD

CB

13(18)19½"

33(46)50cm=

13(18)20cm=5(7)8"

X

19[22]23cm =7½[8½]9"

18[20]20cm =7[8]8"

(OPTIONAL: CUT ALSO LINING FOR VEST)

SIZES: S(M)L
SMALL(MEDIUM)LARGE

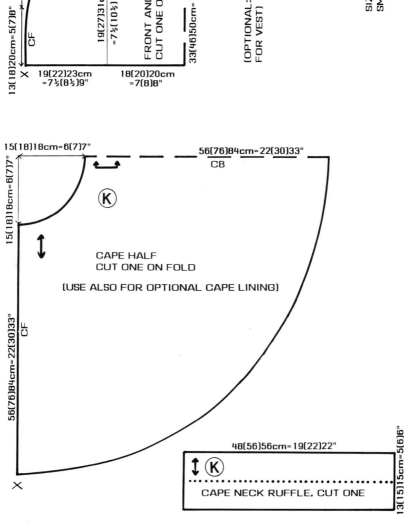

15(18)18cm=6(7)7"

56(76)84cm= 22(30)33"

CB

15(18)18cm=6(7)7"

K

CAPE HALF
CUT ONE ON FOLD

(USE ALSO FOR OPTIONAL CAPE LINING)

56(76)84cm=22(30)33"

CF

X

48(56)56cm=19(22)22"

K

CAPE NECK RUFFLE, CUT ONE

13(15)15cm=5(6)6"

PATTERN L: HOODED ROBE OR CLOAK (Friar, Ghost)

Loose-fitting, hooded robe, shoulders extend into large sleeves. Hooded shoulder cloak for friar. Lightweight cotton-type fabrics for ghost, nonfraying, brown brushed nylon for friar. Fabric required for robe: 180(235)260cm x 115(140)150cm, or 69(92)100" x 45(55)60"; for cloak: 90cm x 90cm, or 36" x 36".

Sewing: Stitch hood top seam; press front edges under and topstitch in place; stitch shoulder seams and then hood seam around neck; stitch sides and underarms. Press hem allowance and sleeve ends under and stitch in place. Cloak: Stitch shoulder seams; stitch hood top seam, press front edges under and topstitch in place and then stitch hood seam around neck.

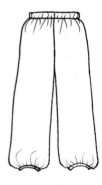

PATTERNS M: BAGGY PANTS OR BLOOMERS, AND TOP (Pants and top for Belly Dancer; pants for Clown, Pierrot; bloomers for Jester)

Very loose-fitting, baggy pants with elasticized waist and ankles; top has shirred front, lace trim, ties around neck. Lightweight cotton-type fabrics; sheer, fancy fabrics for belly dancer. Fabric required for pants: 90(115)130cm x 115(140)150cm, or 35(45)50" x 45(55)60"; for bloomers: 45(50)55cm x 115(140)150cm, or 16(19)21" x 45(55)60"; for top: 50(60)70cm x 90cm, or 20(23)26" x 36". Elastic, lace.

M-1 Baggy pants: Stitch center front and center back seams, then inner leg seams. Sew casings around ankles and waist and insert elastic through casings. Clown: Cut waistline 10cm/4" higher, insert plastic tubing or wire through waist casing, elasticize leg ends. Pierrot: Cut legs 10cm/4" longer; hem lower ends narrowly, stitch stretched elastic around ankles 8cm/3" from lower edge, forming selfruffles. Jester's bloomers have elastic in leg ends.

M-2 Top: Stitch lace all around raw edges. Stitch stretched elastic to center front vertically from bottom to top, shirring the fabric. Stitch center back seam.

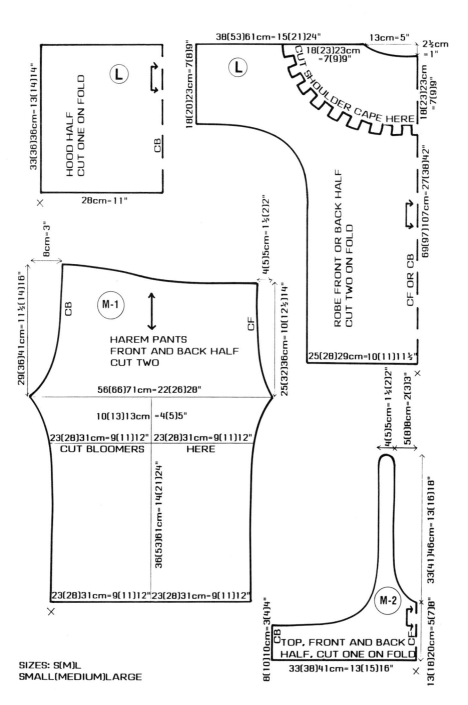

HOOD HALF
CUT ONE ON FOLD

Ⓛ

33(36)36cm=13(14)14"

28cm=11"

CB

38(53)61cm=15(21)24"

13cm=5"

2½cm
=1"

Ⓛ

18(20)23cm=7(8)9"

18(23)23cm
=7(9)9"

CUT SHOULDER CAPE HERE

18(23)23cm
=7(9)9"

ROBE FRONT OR BACK HALF
CUT TWO ON FOLD

CF OR CB

69(97)107cm=27(38)42"

25(28)29cm=10(11)11½"

4(5)5cm=1½(2)2"

8cm=3"

CB

Ⓜ-1

HAREM PANTS
FRONT AND BACK HALF
CUT TWO

CF

29(36)41cm=11½(14)16"

4(5)5cm=1½(2)2"

25(32)36cm=10(12½)14"

56(66)71cm=22(26)28"

10(13)13cm   =4(5)5"

23(28)31cm=9(11)12"   23(28)31cm=9(11)12"

CUT BLOOMERS   HERE

36(53)61cm=14(21)24"

23(28)31cm=9(11)12"   23(28)31cm=9(11)12"

4(5)5cm=1½(2)2"

5(8)8cm=2(3)3"

33(41)46cm=13(16)18"

Ⓜ-2

CB

8(10)10cm=3(4)4"

13(18)20cm=5(7)8"

CE

TOP, FRONT AND BACK
HALF, CUT ONE ON FOLD

33(38)41cm=13(15)16"

SIZES: S(M)L
SMALL(MEDIUM)LARGE

103

PATTERN N: TENTACLES (Octopus)

Eight arms, or tentacles, filled with polyester stuffing, and sewn around pullover ribknit neckband. Lightweight cotton-type fabrics. Fabric required: 90(125)200cm x 140(150)140cm, or 34(48)78" x 55(60)55"; plus ribknit for neckband: 15cm x 50cm, or 6" x 18". Polyester stuffing.

Sewing octopus tentacles: Sew all eight arms closed along both sides, leaving upper ends open; fill with polyester stuffing. Stitch ribknit band into a circle, fold in half right side out and stitch tentacles around it, overlapping each arm a bit to fit around band evenly. Stitch wrist straps made from fabric strips, or wide ribbon, under the two opposite tentacles that fall over child's arms.

PATTERN O: HOODED CAPE (Little Red Ridinghood)

Easy pattern for semi-circular hooded cape with ribbons tied under chin. Mediumweight cotton-type fabrics, velvet, velveteen, corduroy, velour. If you use fabric with one-way nap, reverse the nap so that it runs down on each side. Fabric required: 175(225)240cm x 90(115)115cm, or 68(88)95" x 36(45)45".

Sewing: Stitch center back and hood seams. Overlock front edges and hem allowance, press them narrowly under and topstitch in place. Sew long ribbon around neck leaving ends extending to tie in front. (Add fake fur trimming and lining if desired.)

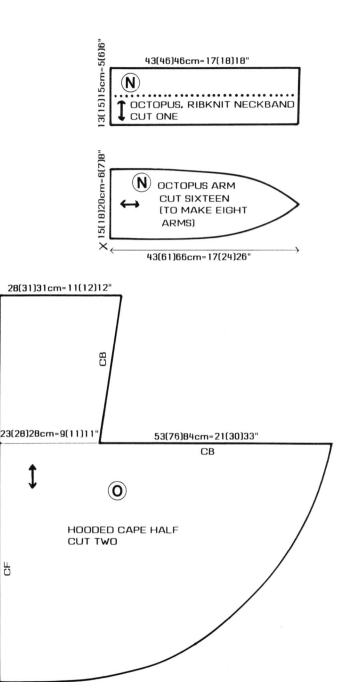

43(46)46cm=17(18)18"

13(15)15cm=5(6)6"

(N)

OCTOPUS, RIBKNIT NECKBAND
CUT ONE

15(18)20cm=6(7)8"

(N) OCTOPUS ARM
CUT SIXTEEN
(TO MAKE EIGHT
ARMS)

X

43(61)66cm=17(24)26"

28(31)31cm=11(12)12"

33(36)36cm=13(14)14"

CB

23(28)28cm=9(11)11"

53(76)84cm=21(30)33"

CB

O

HOODED CAPE HALF
CUT TWO

53(76)84cm=21(30)33"

CF

X

SIZES: S(M)L
SMALL(MEDIUM)LARGE

105

PATTERN P: TUNIC (Peter Pan)

Loose-fitting V-neck tunic with shoulders extending into pointy cap sleeves; also hem edge cut pointy. Felt or other non-fraying fabric, even heavy-duty crepe paper. Fabric required: 55(75)80cm x 115(140)150cm, or 20(28)31" x 45(55)60". Elastic.

Sewing: Stitch shoulder seams (or cut shoulders on fold) and side seams. Stitch stretched elastic around waist. (Crepe paper: Iron seams together with fusible web, or glue with fabric glue. Tie elastic around waist instead of sewing it.)

PATTERNS Q: BARRELS (Pumpkin, Snowman)

Felt. Fabric required for Pumpkin: 60(75)85cm x 200cm, or 22(29)32" x 80". Stiff interfacing: 115(150)165cm x 115cm, or 44(58)64" x 45". Wide bias tape, wire or polyester boning, elastic, black felt scraps. Fabric required for Snowman: 80(95)105cm x 200cm, or 30(36)40" x 80". Stiff interfacing: 115(140)155cm x 115cm, or 45(54)60" x 45". Wide bias tape, elastic, black felt scraps.

Q-1 Pumpkin: Cut sections from felt and interfacing, five of each. Baste interfacing and fabric together. Stitch sections together from neck to hem. Cut armslits in upper edges 20(23)23cm or 8(9)9" long; trim them with bias tape. Sew a bias tape casing in front and back upper edges, and in hem edge; insert elastic through these casings (elastic goes over shoulders). Tack wire or polyester boning around waist on the wrong side of fabric to hold it out from body. Glue or tack on black felt cutouts for facial features.

Q-2 Snowman: Cut sections from felt and interfacing, ten of each. Baste interfacing and fabric together. Stitch five sections together for top half, and remaining five for bottom. Stitch top half to bottom around waist. Fold bias tape in half and stitch it around waist to the seam allowance, forming a casing. Armholes and elasticized casings: see Pumpkin. Insert elastic through waist casing. Glue or tack on black felt "buttons".

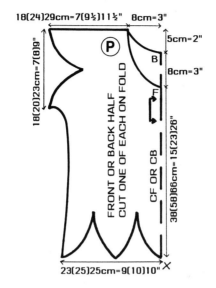

18(24)29cm=7(9½)11½"   8cm=3"

5cm=2"

8cm=3"

18(20)23cm=7(8)9"

P

B

F

FRONT OR BACK HALF
CUT ONE OF EACH ON FOLD

CF OR CB

38(58)66cm=15(23)26"

23(25)25cm=9(10)10"   X

Q-1

25(30½)33cm
= 10(12)13"

PUMPKIN
BARREL SECTION
CUT FIVE

56(74)81cm = 22(29)32"

18(20)23cm = 7(8)9" X

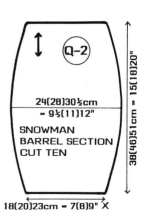

Q-2

24(28)30½cm
= 9½(11)12"

SNOWMAN
BARREL SECTION
CUT TEN

38(46)51cm = 15(18)20"

18(20)23cm = 7(8)9" X

107

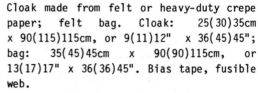

PATTERN R: CLOAK AND BAG (Robin Hood)

Cloak made from felt or heavy-duty crepe paper; felt bag. Cloak: 25(30)35cm x 90(115)115cm, or 9(11)12" x 36(45)45"; bag: 35(45)45cm x 90(90)115cm, or 13(17)17" x 36(36)45". Bias tape, fusible web.

R-1 Cloak: Stitch or glue shoulder seams.
R-2 Bag: Reinforce upper edges with bias tape. Stitch sides and bottom. Fold strap in half lengthwise right side out, and bond layers together by ironing with fusible web sandwiched inside; stitch several parallel lines from end to end. Attach strap ends in place. Optional lining.

PATTERN S: XMAS TREE COSTUME

Felt (or heavy-duty crepe paper; glue sections together to make paper as wide and long as needed). Adjust pattern length to fit child before cutting the fabric. Fabric required: 100(125)cm x 200cm; or 40(48)" x 80". Stiff interfacing: 180(250)cm x 115cm, or 70(96)" x 45". Polyester boning or metal wire: 175(200)cm or 68(80)".

Sewing: Cut two pattern pieces from both felt and interfacing. Stitch interfacing to wrong side of felt around all edges. With right sides out, stitch front to back along edges as shown, leaving bottom open for feet, and leaving openings for hands. Trim the edges close to stitching line. Try the costume on, mark the face opening; take the costume off and cut the face opening. Sew polyester boning or wire around hemline on the wrong side to hold the hem stiff. Decorate the tree with damaged or discarded Christmas ornaments and garlands, or make a few from felt, yarn, crepe and aluminium paper etc.; attach ornaments securely.

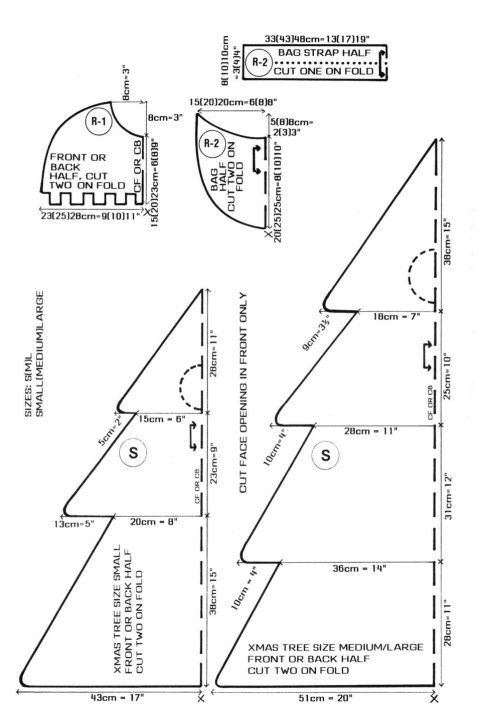

33(43)48cm=13(17)19"

R-2 · BAG STRAP HALF
CUT ONE ON FOLD

8(10)10cm =3(4)4"

R-1

FRONT OR BACK HALF, CUT TWO ON FOLD

8cm=3"
8cm=3"
CF OR CB
15(20)23cm=6(8)9"
23(25)28cm=9(10)11"

15(20)20cm=6(8)8"

R-2

BAG HALF CUT TWO ON FOLD

5(8)8cm= 2(3)3"
20(25)25cm=8(10)10"

SIZES: S(M)L
SMALL(MEDIUM)LARGE

S

XMAS TREE SIZE SMALL FRONT OR BACK HALF CUT TWO ON FOLD

5cm=2"
15cm = 6"
13cm=5"
20cm = 8"
28cm=11"
23cm=9"
38cm = 15"
CF OR CB
43cm = 17"

CUT FACE OPENING IN FRONT ONLY

S

XMAS TREE SIZE MEDIUM/LARGE FRONT OR BACK HALF CUT TWO ON FOLD

9cm=3½"
18cm = 7"
10cm=4"
28cm = 11"
10cm=4"
36cm = 14"
38cm=15"
25cm=10"
31cm=12"
28cm=11"
CF OR CB
51cm = 20"

PATTERNS T: WINGS

T-1 Angel: Cut angel wings from white poster board. Make small holes as shown; attach elastic arm straps or long ribbons through holes to tie around shoulders.

T-2 Bat; T-3 Bumblebee: Cut bat wings from black poster board, and bumblebee wings from yellow poster board (see angel).

T-3 Elf; T-4 Fairy: Crepe paper or lightweight, cotton-type fabrics, tulle, chiffon, etc. Double-layered. Outline pattern on crepe paper or fabric, but don't cut it out yet; drizzle a thin layer of craft glue (such as Velcro Adhesive; follow package directions carefully) along pattern outline, press flexible wire into glue, and then press another sheet of crepe paper or fabric on top. Let dry; then cut off the excess paper or fabric around wire. (Test first with scraps to get the hang of this method.) Make two small holes where shown, insert elastic ribbons through holes for armstraps. Glue the ribbons in place for added strength.

T-5 Butterfly: Two separate sheets of poster board, front and back cut alike. Adjust the pattern to fit your child. Glue or paint colorful designs on wings. Cut small holes through both layers, and attach ribbons through holes to tie front and back together at waist and shoulders.

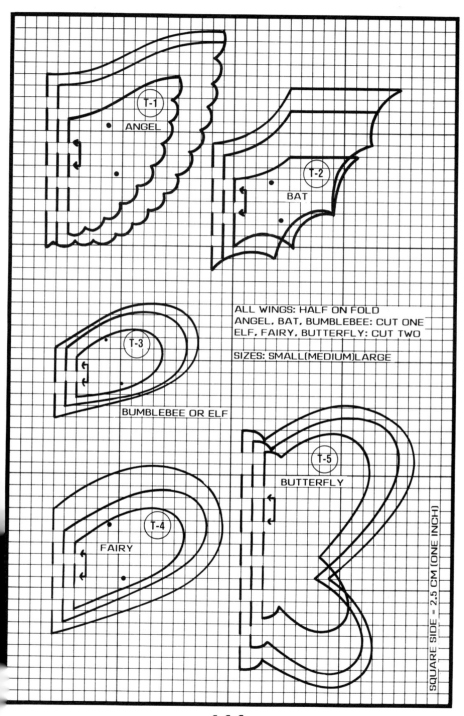

T-1 ANGEL

T-2 BAT

T-3

BUMBLEBEE OR ELF

ALL WINGS: HALF ON FOLD
ANGEL, BAT, BUMBLEBEE: CUT ONE
ELF, FAIRY, BUTTERFLY: CUT TWO

SIZES: SMALL(MEDIUM)LARGE

T-4 FAIRY

T-5 BUTTERFLY

SQUARE SIDE = 2.5 CM (ONE INCH)

PATTERN U: BODYSUIT (African Dancer, Ballerina, Belly Dancer, Elf, Hawaiian Hula Dancer)

Close-fitting bodysuit, long sleeves. Two-way stretch knits only, such as spandex. The patterns are for small and medium sizes; easy to enlarge for large size. Fabric required: 45(60)cm x 115(140)cm, or 17(22)" x 45(55)". Elastic.

Sewing: Stitch shoulder seams. Stitch sleeves to bodice, then stitch sides, underarms, and crotch seam. Hem sleeve ends narrowly. Zigzag slightly stretched narrow elastic to neck edge and legholes on the wrong side of fabric, turn elasticized edges under and zigzag in place.

PATTERNS V: TUTU & SLIPPERS (Ballerina)

Short, double-layered skirt (from tulle, net, or other sheer, non-fraying fabric) ruffled around waist. Bodice from stretch knits only, such as spandex; elasticized shirring on front. Slippers without soles are designed to be worn over sneakers; ribbons tied around ankles. The patterns are for small and medium sizes; easy to enlarge for large size. Fabric required for bodice and slippers: 40(40)cm x 115(140)cm, or 14(19)" x 45(55)"; for double-layered skirt: 35(55)cm x 150(160)cm, or 14(22)" x 60(64)". Lace, elastic, sequins, bias tape, ribbons.

V-1 Tutu: Stitch shoulder seams. Trim armholes and neck with lace. Zigzag 5cm/2" piece of stretched elastic vertically to center front, shirring the fabric. Stitch side seams. Stitch the two skirt sections together into a circle (add more skirt layers, if desired); gather upper edges (each one separately), and stitch them to the lower edge of bodice. Sew or glue sequins on bodice and skirt.

V-2 Slippers: Zigzag stretched elastic to both upper and lower edges, stitch center front seams, turn elasticized edges under and stitch in place. Stitch long ribbons to each side to tie around ankles. Add elastic straps under feet.

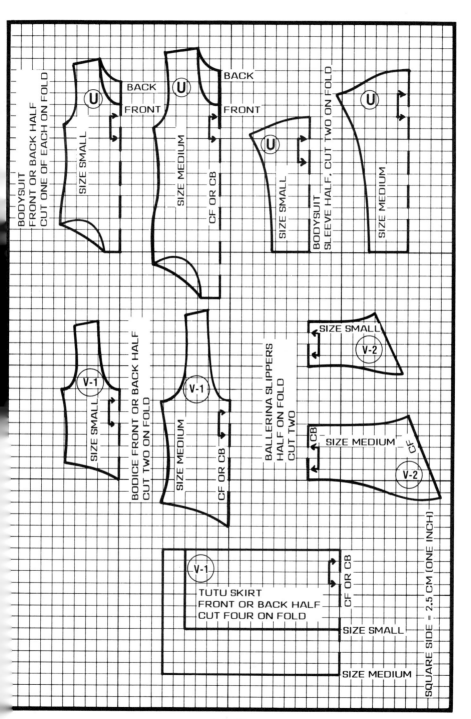

BODYSUIT
FRONT OR BACK HALF
CUT ONE OF EACH ON FOLD

SIZE SMALL

BACK
FRONT

SIZE MEDIUM

CF OR CB

BACK
FRONT

BODYSUIT SLEEVE HALF. CUT TWO ON FOLD

SIZE SMALL

SIZE MEDIUM

BODICE FRONT OR BACK HALF
CUT TWO ON FOLD

SIZE SMALL

SIZE MEDIUM

CF OR CB

BALLERINA SLIPPERS
HALF ON FOLD
CUT TWO

SIZE SMALL

V-2

CB

SIZE MEDIUM

CF

V-2

TUTU SKIRT
FRONT OR BACK HALF
CUT FOUR ON FOLD

V-1

CF OR CB

SIZE SMALL

SIZE MEDIUM

SQUARE SIDE = 2.5 CM (ONE INCH)

113

W-1 Hood (Bat, Bunny, Cat, Devil, Mouse): Ear patterns for hood on facing page, horns for devil from Viking pattern W-18. Stiffen ear pieces with interfacing or batting (or, after sewing ears ready, stiffen them with pipe cleaners, so that pipe cleaner ends will be stitched between the side slits of hood to hold ears up); fill horns with polyester stuffing. Sew ears or horns ready, turn right side out, and stitch them between side slits of hood. Stitch center panel between side panels (fabric and lining separately). Stitch lining and hood together around front edge; turn right side out. Topstitch front edge. Cut a fabric strip (10x48cm, or 4x19") for neckband; stitch ends under, fold the band in half lengthwise right side out and stitch it to hood's lower edge, leaving band ends open to form a casing; insert wide ribbon through casing to tie at front; stitch ribbon to casing center back to prevent it from slipping out.

W-2 Balaclava helmet (Bumblebee, Butterfly, Gingerbread Man, Skeleton, Tree): Stretchy fabrics only. Stitch center back and center front seams. Overlock lower edge. Turn helmet inside out. Stitch ribknit band into a circle, fold in half right side out and stitch it around face opening.

W-3 Cone-shaped hat (Clown, Fairy, Gnome, Santa Claus, Witch): Fabric or poster board. Stitch or glue center back seam. Hem lower edge narrowly, if the hat is made of fabric. Trims as shown on costume pages. Witch: Cut brim and crown from poster board; clip brim's inner edge, fold clipped edge upward and glue to inside of crown. Add elastic chinstrap.

W-4 Brim hat (Drummer, Toy Soldier): Poster board. Glue crown into a circle. Clip brim's inner edge, fold clipped edge upward and glue to inside of crown. Add elastic chinstrap.

W-5 Petal face (Flower): Poster board. Glue petals between the two layers of circular front bands, spacing the petals evenly. Sew or staple a T-shaped elastic strap to hold the headwear in place at back of head (use bobby pins if necessary).

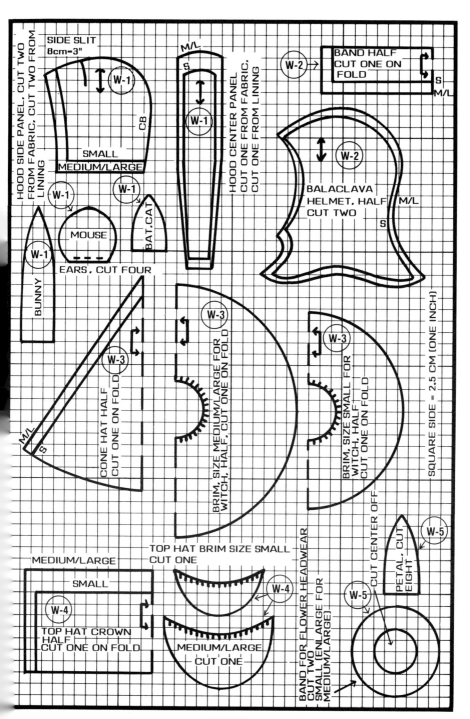

HOOD SIDE PANEL, CUT TWO FROM FABRIC. CUT TWO FROM LINING

SIDE SLIT 8cm–3"

W-1

CB

SMALL
MEDIUM/LARGE

W-1

W-1

MOUSE

BAT.CAT

W-1

BUNNY

EARS, CUT FOUR

M/L
S

W-1

HOOD CENTER PANEL.
CUT ONE FROM FABRIC.
CUT ONE FROM LINING

W-2

BAND HALF
CUT ONE ON
FOLD

S
M/L

W-2

BALACLAVA
HELMET, HALF
CUT TWO

M/L
S

W-3

BRIM, SIZE MEDIUM/LARGE FOR
WITCH, HALF. CUT ONE ON FOLD

W-3

CONE HAT HALF
CUT ONE ON FOLD

M/L
S

W-3

BRIM, SIZE SMALL FOR
WITCH, HALF. CUT ONE ON FOLD

SQUARE SIDE = 2.5 CM (ONE INCH)

MEDIUM/LARGE

SMALL

W-4

TOP HAT CROWN
HALF
CUT ONE ON FOLD

TOP HAT BRIM SIZE SMALL
CUT ONE

W-4

MEDIUM/LARGE
CUT ONE

BAND FOR FLOWER HEADWEAR
CUT TWO
SMALL (ENLARGE FOR
MEDIUM/LARGE)

W-5

CUT CENTER OFF

W-5

PETAL, CUT
EIGHT

W-5

115

W-6 Cap (Clown, Jailbird, Pierrot, Pumpkin, wig basecap): Both stretchy and non-stretchy fabrics. Stitch side slits closed. Sew stretched elastic around lower edge, turn it under and stitch in place.

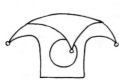

W-7 Three-pointed Hat (Jester): Baste or iron interfacing to wrong side of fabric. Stitch center back seam of lower section, then sew lower section to upper section matching the three points. Fill tips lightly with polyester stuffing. Attach small bell to each point. If using fabric that frays, trim face opening with bias tape and hem lower edge narrowly.

W-8 Fool's sceptre hat: Stitch center back seam of lower section and then sew it to upper section around all points (as for hat above).

W-9 Neck ruffle (Jester): (Use interfacing for soft fabric.) Stitch both layers together around points, leaving neck open. Clip corners, turn right side out, and press. Stitch ribknit band into a circle, fold in half lengthwise right side out and stitch it around neck, stretching the band to divide fullness evenly. Sew small bell to each point.

W-10 Helmet (Knight): Poster board. Glue crown's back seam. Glue neckguard into a circle. Clip crown's lower edge as shown, and glue clipped edge inside upper edge of neckguard. Cover helmet with aluminium paper. Draw tiny circles all over with black permanent marker. Attach a feather on top. Add elastic chinstrap.

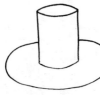

W-11 Tophat (Magician, Peppermint Candy, Snowman): Poster board. Glue crown into a circle. (Large size: Trim 1.3cm/½" off from brim's inner edge.) Clip brim's inner edge as shown, fold clipped edge upward and glue inside crown. Add chinstrap.

W-12 Hat (Peter Pan): Felt. Stitch side seams. Turn brim upward at the back and attach a feather to it. Add elastic chinstrap.

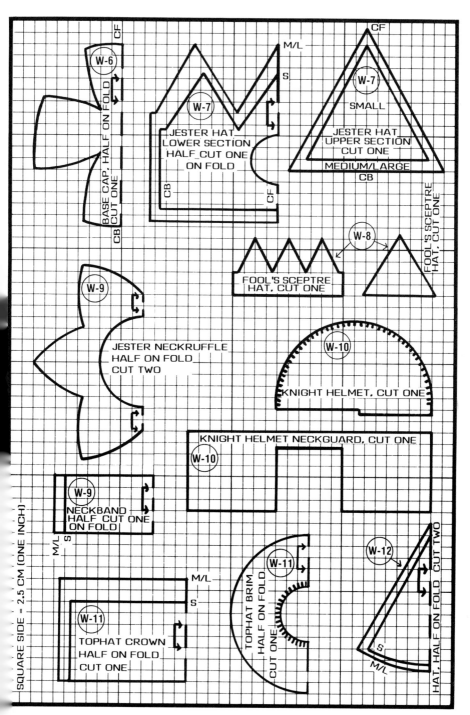

SQUARE SIDE = 2.5 CM (ONE INCH)

W-6
BASE CAP, HALF ON FOLD
CUT ONE
CF
CB

M/L
S

W-7
JESTER HAT
LOWER SECTION
HALF CUT ONE
ON FOLD
CB
CF

CF
W-7
SMALL
JESTER HAT
UPPER SECTION
CUT ONE
MEDIUM/LARGE
CB

W-8
FOOL'S SCEPTRE
HAT, CUT ONE

FOOL'S SCEPTRE
HAT, CUT ONE

W-9
JESTER NECKRUFFLE
HALF ON FOLD
CUT TWO

W-10
KNIGHT HELMET, CUT ONE

KNIGHT HELMET NECKGUARD, CUT ONE
W-10

W-9
NECKBAND
HALF CUT ONE
ON FOLD

M/L
S

W-11
TOPHAT CROWN
HALF ON FOLD
CUT ONE

M/L
S

W-11
TOPHAT BRIM
HALF ON FOLD
CUT ONE

W-12
HAT, HALF ON FOLD, CUT TWO
S
M/L

117

W-13 Hat (Robin Hood): Felt. Stitch side seam and top. Stitch brim into a circle and then around crown. Fold brim upward at back, add a feather. Add elastic chinstrap.

W-14 Star: Poster board. Glue the two layers together around points, leaving neck open as shown. Face opening on front.

W-15 Crown (Princess): Glue gold metallic paper on poster board, cut the pattern out, glue or staple back seam together. Add elastic chinstrap.

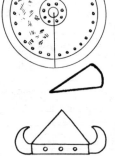

W-16 Shield (Viking): Gray poster board. Slightly overlap circle ends to give shield convex shape; glue together. Decorate with black marker. Glue a strip of poster board onto the back for handle.

W-17 Nose (Snowman, Witch): Poster board or felt. Glue long sides together.

W-18 Helmet (Viking): Gray poster board. Glue crown's back seam. Glue band into a circle, clip crown's lower edge and glue the clipped edge under band. Horns from white poster board, felt or crepe paper; glue each horn around edges, leaving lower end open; fill tips lightly with polyester stuffing. Cut a hole in both sides of band, push horns through, clip lower edges of horns, bend the clipped edge and glue to inside of band.

PATTERNS X: MITTENS AND GLOVES

X-1 Mittens (Bumblebee, Bunny, Cat, Mouse, Gingerbread Man, Gnome, Santa Claus, Snowman): Same fabrics as for costume. Stitch around all edges and thumb. Stitch casing at wrist, and insert elastic through casing. (Optional lining.)

X-2 Gloves (Ghost, Magician, Mummy, Pierrot, Skeleton): Stretchy fabrics only, such as cotton knit. Draw pattern by placing hand on paper, with fingers open; draw around fingers, add generous seam allowances. Stitch with short, narrow zigzag. Turn wrist edge under. Stitch a short piece of stretched elastic at wrist crease.

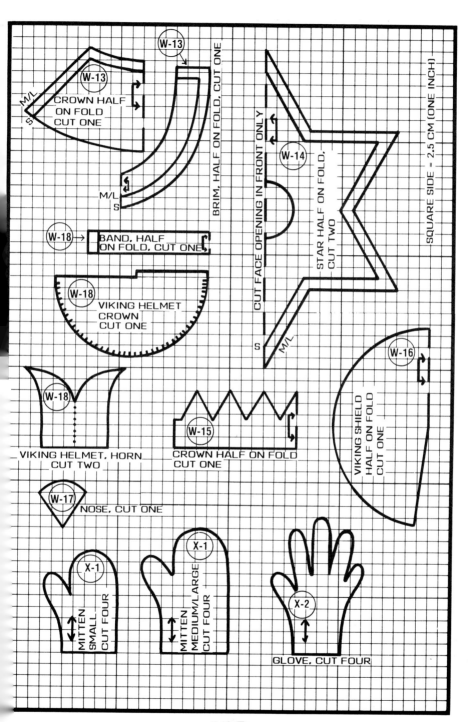

W-13

W-13 CROWN HALF ON FOLD CUT ONE

M/L S

M/L S

BRIM, HALF ON FOLD, CUT ONE

W-18 → BAND, HALF ON FOLD, CUT ONE

W-18 VIKING HELMET CROWN CUT ONE

CUT FACE OPENING IN FRONT ONLY

W-14 STAR HALF ON FOLD, CUT TWO

S M/L

SQUARE SIDE = 2.5 CM (ONE INCH)

W-18 VIKING HELMET, HORN CUT TWO

W-15 CROWN HALF ON FOLD CUT ONE

W-16 VIKING SHIELD HALF ON FOLD CUT ONE

W-17 NOSE, CUT ONE

X-1 MITTEN SMALL CUT FOUR

X-1 MITTEN MEDIUM/LARGE CUT FOUR

X-2 GLOVE, CUT FOUR

PATTERNS Y: SPATS

Y-1 Fabric spats (Bunny, Cat, Mouse): Same fabrics as for costume. Hem lower edge. Sew bias tape casing to upper edge; insert elastic through casing, pull it up and stitch ends securely to casing ends. Stitch center front seam. Attach elastic straps under feet.

Y-2 Fabric spats with curvy toes (Jester, Peter Pan, Robin Hood): Felt or heavy-duty crepe paper, plus stiff interfacing. Stitch or glue center front seam and around curvy tip. Fill pointy front tips with polyester stuffing. Attach elastic straps under feet. Tie elastic around ankles to keep spats in place.

Y-3 Poster board spats (Cowboy): Punch two holes in both back edges. Insert cords through holes to tie the spats at back. Decorate spats with markers.

Y-4 Knee-high poster board spats (Indian, Knight, Pirate, Santa Claus, Toy Soldier, Viking): Punch four holes in both back edges for cords to tie them at back.

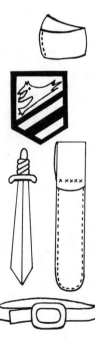

PATTERNS Z: ACCESSORIES

Z-1 Gun case (Cowboy): Fake or real leather or suede. Stitch belt carrier to the wider end on the right side as shown; stitch case ends together.

Z-2 Crest (Knight): Cut from gray cardboard, decorate with black marker.

Z-3 Sword (Knight, Pirate, Viking): Cardboard, decorated with black marker or covered with aluminium paper.

Z-4 Scabbard (Knight, Pirate, Viking): Gray felt or poster board. Stitch or glue front to back around edges; fold scabbard upper edge back where shown and tack or glue closed, forming a large loop for belt.

Z-5 Belt and buckle (Knight, Viking): Knight belt: Fold felt in half lengthwise, bond layers together with fusible web; stitch from end to end. Cut the buckle from plastic (such as a large plastic container lid), cover with aluminium paper; insert one end of belt through buckle, turn around center bar and sew in place. Viking: Glue gray poster board belt in half lengthwise, decorate with black marker; attach with safety pin; scabbard will cover the pin.

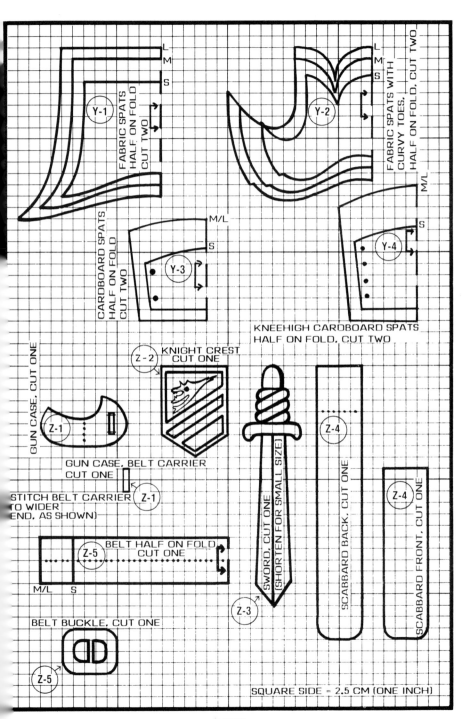

L
M
S

Y-1

FABRIC SPATS
HALF ON FOLD
CUT TWO

CARDBOARD SPATS
HALF ON FOLD
CUT TWO

L
M
S

Y-2

FABRIC SPATS WITH
CURVY TOES.
HALF ON FOLD. CUT TWO

M/L

M/L
S

Y-3

S

Y-4

KNEEHIGH CARDBOARD SPATS
HALF ON FOLD. CUT TWO

GUN CASE. CUT ONE

Z-1

GUN CASE, BELT CARRIER
CUT ONE

STITCH BELT CARRIER **Z-1**
(TO WIDER
END. AS SHOWN)

Z-2
KNIGHT CREST
CUT ONE

Z-5
BELT HALF ON FOLD.
CUT ONE

M/L   S

BELT BUCKLE. CUT ONE

Z-5

Z-3
SWORD. CUT ONE
(SHORTEN FOR SMALL SIZE)

Z-4

SCABBARD BACK. CUT ONE

Z-4

SCABBARD FRONT. CUT ONE

SQUARE SIDE = 2.5 CM (ONE INCH)

MORE COSTUME IDEAS

Although this book contains many good ideas for children's costumes and props, they are just a few of the innumerable possibilities. If you are likely to need lots of costume ideas, start collecting them. Whenever you see a suitable idea for a costume in a magazine or on television, cut it out or make a simple sketch so you won't forget it. Save all collected ideas in a big envelope. You will treasure your envelope when the next Halloween or masquerade party comes around.

Some good sources to collect more costume ideas:

Advertisements and magazine articles during Halloween.

Toddlers' books, children's illustrated encyclopedias and history books.

Travel agent's brochures of exotic destinations showing native peoples.

Ask kids; they can come up with amazing ideas (many costumes and details in this book came from my own children).

Look at children trick-or-treating on Halloween; take snapshots of the best ideas, or sketch them.

Next time you watch a parade or circus on TV, keep a note book and pen at hand to jot down any ideas you feel could be used for homemade costumes. The costumes and accessories in televised parades are so beautiful and professional that is is hard to reproduce them at home especially with a tight budget. However, such a huge selection of ideas is sure to spark your imagination to simplify a few of them for your own use.

BE A PART OF MY BOOKS

I am constantly reprinting my books and occasionally revising them. Realizing that some of the best ideas might come from my innovative readers, I am inviting your contributions.

If you have costume ideas for children or adults, or great sewing tips that you would like to share with my readers, I would love to hear from you. Send me a simple drawing or a snapshot and any necessary details. If I use your idea, I will send you a complimentary, autographed copy of that book. Send ideas to: Leila Albala, P.O. Box 203, Chambly, Quebec J3L 4B3, Canada.

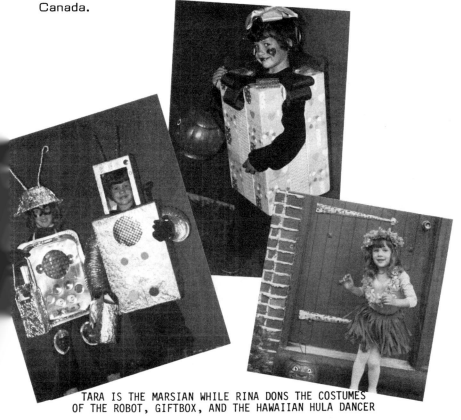

TARA IS THE MARSIAN WHILE RINA DONS THE COSTUMES OF THE ROBOT, GIFTBOX, AND THE HAWAIIAN HULA DANCER

INDEX

(Photographs: See pages 1, 4, 21, 22, 23, 123, 127, 128)

ALBERT DONS THE COSTUMES OF THE GALAXY KID, THE SKELETON, AND THE JAILBIRD, WHILE RINA IS DRESSED UP AS THE CLOWN, THE GNOME, AND THE BUTTERFLY.

GLIMPSES OF THE AUTHOR

From her childhood days in rural Finland, making tiny garments for dolls, through teen years sewing her own designs for friends, and on to adult life designing and sewing for pleasure and business, Leila Albala has combined her love of creative sewing with practical wearability. Upon graduation from Finnish commercial college, Leila worked in several European countries, gaining experience in a variety of jobs. When she and her husband, Elie, came to Canada in 1973, they founded their own mail order business, named ALPEL. Their self publishing business started in 1982. While sewing constantly for her children, Albert and Rina, Leila developed her own patterns and an easy way to design and print them in miniature. Her first book, "Easy Sewing for Infants", became an instant success after it was featured in Family Circle, Vogue Patterns, and dozens of other magazines. Thereafter, positive feedback from her readers inspired Leila to continue the series with "Easy Sewing for Children", "Easy Sewing for Adults", and "Easy Halloween Costumes for Children".

128